TOWARD A GENERAL THEORY OF HUMAN JUDGMENT

by
Justus Buchler

SECOND, REVISED EDITION

DOVER PUBLICATIONS, INC.
NEW YORK

TO

THE MEMORY OF MY MOTHER

IDA FROST BUCHLER

Published in Canada by General Publishing Company, Ltd.,
30 Lesmill Road, Don Mills, Toronto, Ontario.
Published in the United Kingdom by Constable and Company,
Ltd., 10 Orange Street, London WC2H 7EG.

This Dover edition, first published in 1979, is an unabridged
and revised republication of the work originally published by Columbia University Press in 1951 under the same title.

International Standard Book Number: 0-486-23874-1
Library of Congress Catalog Card Number: 79-51886

Manufactured in the United States of America
Dover Publications, Inc.
180 Varick Street
New York, N.Y. 10014

CONTENTS

PREFACE TO
THE DOVER EDITION

THIS BOOK (TGT), first published in 1951, is the original and perhaps still the most desirable entrance to what I have since called a metaphysics of the human process. Its concepts aim to discern the broadest and deepest aspects of human functioning. Stating such an aim is itself a delicate step; yet imperfections have not diminished the philosophic importance and growing acceptance of the effort involved.

When the book appeared its favorable impact was accompanied by a felt need on the part of readers for elaboration. I had anticipated this aspect of the response by promising "future studies." Undoubtedly, readers were expressing their incipient and willing engagement with a framework of unfamiliar ideas. But I soon found that they were also expressing the difficulty they had in assimilating the exposition. Portions of the book are written as if I had already discussed the main ideas with all who might be interested, and could therefore rely on them to supply connections and draw implications taken for granted by me. The present edition cannot reverse an earlier spirit of composition. And probably this is all to the good; for I would not want, by means of a few expedient simplifications, to dim whatever insights have been due to that spirit. In the years following, four more books appeared, building from the impetus of TGT, placing its ideas within a general ontology, and reflecting anew the conception of philosophy by which the entire series is animated.*

The later books, far from supplanting TGT, reveal its indispensability to the structure that all have shaped. Aside from certain central ideas which continue to be defined and applied, most of its major topics are not taken up again. Because of this fact, and because so much is begun or foreshadowed by TGT, the subsequent developments gain firmer meaning when referred back to it as conceptual progenitor.

We are led by TGT in two directions. In one, we continue to investigate invariant and variant traits of the human process. In the other, we move toward a wider metaphysics that delineates the more pervasive settings of this process. A metaphysics of the human process makes clear the need for a metaphysics of natural complexes—man being one among innumerable complexes of nature, some of which are *not* processes. From the vantage ground of the present, TGT actually may be seen to suggest that we cannot adequately understand the human process itself if we think of it as constituted only by processes. The book introduces the concept "natural complex," which

---

* With their abbreviations (required for reference in the Appendix), they are:

NJ: *Nature and Judgment*. New York: Columbia University Press, 1955.
CM: *The Concept of Method*. Columbia, 1961.
MNC: *Metaphysics of Natural Complexes*. Columbia, 1966.
ML: *The Main of Light: On the Concept of Poetry*. New York: Oxford University Press, 1974.

later, among its other functions, is of ontological importance as the means of identifying generically whatever we can discriminate or whatever we wish to categorize.

A problem which faced earlier readers of TGT was its rather unconventional plunge at the outset into starkly theoretical considerations. One can sympathize with a reader who would want to know more about the historical background of viewpoints which appear to be presupposed and are not dealt with in the opening chapter. In 1951 I felt that the book's direct, non-polemical approach could be accepted on its own terms, simply as a way of looking at man in the world, and without answering to the beck of traditional "issues." I now perceive that the beginning of the book is more polemical than I had at first thought.

Accordingly, in this edition I have provided an Introduction designed to help orient readers to the main idea of the first chapter, proception. The idea of proception underlies and yields the idea of utterance or judgment; and the latter, as here transformed from its persistent, restricted historical sense, is basic to a metaphysics of man. At the other end of the book I have added a short Appendix, which singles out for comment a number of expressions or allusions in the text.

The two hundred or so verbal changes made in this edition are limited to the replacement of words or phrases, and cannot be called substantive revisions. They contribute, I feel, to accuracy or precision of intent. Some may be scarcely noticed, others will make a difference in sense or difference in emphasis.

J. B.

January, 1979

PREFACE TO
THE ORIGINAL EDITION

I MIGHT HAVE DESCRIBED this essay as a metaphysics of utterance, were it not for the mischievous associations of the former term and the narrowness of the province suggested by the latter. For me the present title is of equivalent import, and it is probably less offensive if more prosaic. These pages attempt to lay a conceptual foundation for the understanding of such phenomena as symbolism and language, meaning and representation, communication and method. Every theory aims, in the last analysis, to exhibit a structure among data ordinarily regarded as disparate: by the use of a relatively small number of categories a scheme is devised which requires to be self-consistent and consistent with other schemes that have come to be thought part of the fabric of knowledge. The burden that a philosophic theory in particular bears is likely to be great; for beyond these primal requirements it dedicates itself to the difficult union of a high level of generality with interpretative justice. In the case of such a theory the circumstances of verification are usually very complex, and the acceptability of the result depends ultimately, perhaps, upon the presence of a sense of philosophic satisfaction in the reader, who is both spectator and participant.

The present approach uses as expedient the notion of utterance or judgment: the principal problem is to define the generic conditions and properties of the human product. By a product I understand anything at all (any instance of making, doing, or saying) that issues from human life or human relationship, and I conceive of every product as a judgment—in the sense which the sequel describes. The terms and notions here employed are in large measure implicitly defined by contexts subsequent to those in which they are introduced. Even so, they remain in need of amplification. I am aware that in what follows many more questions are raised than are answered. I have kept this book brief in the expectation that the structure may emerge the more fully. The obligation to elaborate I hope to satisfy through future studies.

J. B.

NEW YORK
MARCH, 1951

ACKNOWLEDGMENTS

I am glad for the opportunity to record here the intellectual and moral benefit that has come to me from association with my friend and teacher John H. Randall, Jr. His power to identify with the ideas of others, and to fuse sympathy with critical severity, I have experienced many times, but most particularly in a graduate seminar at Columbia that he and I have given jointly for the past few years.

Besides Professor Randall, three colleagues have favored me with comments on the manuscript. Professor Herbert W. Schneider has raised various knotty problems of terminology. Professor James Gutmann has suggested useful changes in formulation. Professor Jacques Barzun has not only saved me from some serious ambiguities but has prevented me in several instances from misrepresenting my own intent.

To my wife, Professor Evelyn Shirk of Hofstra College, I owe many insights derived from discussion of the philosophic issues that both of us have felt to be important.

INTRODUCTION

We are inclined to think of philosophic concepts as located in philosophic discourse, and as acquiring their meaning in that type of context. But there are certain concepts which occupy a conspicuous place both in philosophic thought and in everyday speech. Prime examples are knowledge, goodness, existence, and experience. Terms like these, which have as it were a dual career, are often crucial and pivotal. But the concept of experience differs from the others in a remarkable way. For unlike them, it has been very little debated by philosophers so far as its meaning is concerned. Philosophers have argued extensively the nature of knowledge, its conditions, its forms. They have asked repeatedly how goodness is determined. They have disputed about what can be said to "exist." But they have seldom worried about their own or others' use of "experience." They treat the notion as if it had an obvious and universal meaning. Sometimes they will extol and sometimes disparage it; in either case, mainly for its instrumental role toward the clarification of another concept, like knowledge. Thus they will evaluate the relative importance of that which they do not find it necessary to clarify. And they deal with it as if normalcy required them to keep it away from close consideration. Not only do most philosophers seem unaware of the diversity of meanings which the concept actually has acquired; they seem unaware of the theoretic consequences which these different meanings entail. One reason why they pay scant attention to a comparative treatment of experience is that their own version, being implicit and not directly articulated, is unavailable for comparison. I say "most philosophers"; some, of course, have reflected not only explicitly but acutely on their own usage and intent. But whether implicit or explicit, *some* conception of experience is in fact used or presupposed or depended on by every philosopher.

I am going to consider a number of influential conceptions that can be extracted from major philosophic outlooks. The aim is necessarily a limited one. Basically, it is twofold: first, to convey a sense of the complications in the notion as such—in the term and concept "experience"; and second, to indicate the kind of problems inherent in each of the viewpoints selected.

At the outset, one possible confusion may be anticipated. It concerns the relation between the concept of experience and the doctrine of empiricism. Actually there is no more of a significant connection between "experience" and "empiricism" than between experience and any other doctrine. What have been labelled as "mysticism" and "rationalism" or any other "ism" all entail some conception of experience, whatever their position may be about the role of experience in the world or in the world of man. And what these positions, including empiricism, mean will be affected by what "experience" is taken to mean. It may or may not be true that so-called empiricists talk more about experience, or use the word more, than others do. But they have devoted as little effort to clarifying it as their opponents have. Thus Locke, after a high-sounding statement about experience early in his *Essay Concerning Human Understanding*, seldom uses the term again in that great and lengthy work. By contrast Kant, who would not be called an empiricist without strong qualification, speaks of experience on almost every page of the *Critique of Pure Reason*. Yet neither Locke nor Kant spends time wondering whether the term as he uses it might be troublesome, ambiguous, or evasive in its implications, or what differing effects it might have on the general interpretation of his position.

Let us consider certain typical, and one or two untypical, ways in which the term occurs. Among the following examples, some are characteristic of everyday, others of philosophic, discourse.

(1) "That was a dreadful experience." In this usage, experience is something more or less limited and localized. At the same time, it is far less limited than perception is ordinarily thought to be. We would not typically say "That was a dreadful perception," although it might be supposed, with whatever justification, that the experience is nothing but a sum of perceptions.

(2) "Never in all my experience has this happened." In this usage experience is not something limited and localized. It is something extended, stretched out, certainly in time and possibly in space as well. It stems

from the past and is vaguely presumed to continue in the future. Often it is given a name in recognition of traits that represent it, or in recognition of its social character. Thus: "She has been close to the Black Experience."

(3) "Your experience as a carpenter is greater than mine." Here we have an implication of what is not present in either of the two preceding usages, namely degree. Experience admits of more and less. Uniqueness is irrelevant. And there is yet another implication that usually seems to reside in the mere statement of comparison—the suggestion of more experience being in some sense better than less.

(4) "You may think this way, but experience shows otherwise." A generalized version of this usage would be: "All our beliefs ought to be tested in experience." A familiar version is: "Experience is the best teacher." Here experience is not something limited (as in the first usage); it is not something belonging to me, an individual, and continuing to belong to me (as in the second usage); it is not something of which a greater amount is better than a lesser (as in the third usage). It is rather something to which we turn, and to which we turn in a certain way. We turn to some aspect of the world that is independent of us. In another sense correlative to this one, what we turn to (in the sense of resorting to) is an activity, say the activity of experimenting, or the activity of observing through "the senses." Even more than this is implied. For it is not your or my turning, not what you or I observe, but what anyone would observe or have to observe.

"Experience" in this usage, then, entails a method and a norm. It is something to which we appeal, and which adjudicates, but to which we may not wish to appeal or do not.

(5) "That is what dramatists have found important in human experience." Here experience is not what one decides to consult or appeal to or recall. It is what one is involved in whether one chooses to be or not. This generic and social orientation implies recurrences in human life, patterns of a sort. But it does not exclude the unusual if that too comes to be recognized as "human." In the rhetorical addition of the latter word we are thinking of experience not merely as extensive but as pervasive. In a sense it is part of each individual. But in a sense which equally well fits this usage, each individual is a part of it. The social factor here lies not only in what many share, but in the way they share it.

(6) "Experience is knowledge by means of connected perceptions." This is a statement by Kant. It reflects a general view of experience as having two sides: (*a*) as the impact that "objects" (including our own self) make on us—as appearances that we "sense"; and (*b*) as the laws, the conditions, inherent in the knowing faculty, through which that faculty structures—connects—these appearances. Kant, however, is not consistent or unvarying in his use of "experience," possibly because he often needs to select or emphasize one of its aspects. Thus he will use it sometimes to mean mere sensory impact from "without"; sometimes to mean knowledge of the kind that is limited to the accumulation of particular

sensory perceptions; sometimes to mean the entire extent of what can appear to a knower by virtue of the connecting cognitive forms which organize the "raw materials" of sense. The phrase "given in experience," itself far from clear but extremely widespread in modern philosophy, is typically Kantian. Kant believes, for example, that we can "think" some kinds of "objects" which are not objects of *experience*, which cannot be *given* in experience. Many philosophers use "experiencing" and "sensing" interchangeably.

(7) "Education is the continuous reconstruction of experience." These are the words of John Dewey. There is nothing unusual about each of them taken individually. But there is something quite unusual about the statement as a whole, and no simple meaning can be provided for it. The larger context of which it is part needs to be explicated, including Dewey's view of education; that is not possible here. What I shall try to do, a little later, is to define the general character of Dewey's approach to experience. Then the reader can try to figure out independently where in the general scheme the quoted use of "experience" might fit.

At this point it seems desirable to concentrate attention on philosophers and philosophic contexts. But with whom should we start? If we asked our next-door neighbor whom he thought of when the word "experience" was spoken, he would probably name his grandfather, or some aged and venerable person in public life. But if our neighbor happened to be a philosopher, he would probably say "Hume!" And I am quite willing to fall in line, even if not for the same reason.

Now one of Hume's dominant interests, of course, was to explain what it means for a belief to be justified, to be valid. He was especially interested in those beliefs which were not limited by their relevance to what he called "the present testimony of our senses, or the records of our memory." His familiar position, that no amount of reasoning, but rather experience alone, can give these beliefs whatever validity they have, does not concern us. What does concern us is the way in which his problem is couched, and the meaning which it yields for the notion of experience. Take the phrase "the present testimony of our senses, or the records of our memory." If we turn away for a moment from the most widely heralded word in this phrase, namely "senses," we surely must be struck by the two metaphors "testimony" and "records." The senses give testimony, the memory keeps the record. These are legal metaphors, metaphors imported from legal procedure. Hume is telling us that sensing is a kind of evidence. But the essential point is that no evidence can be substantial which consists in only a single instance of testimony. Testimony must be duplicated, corroborated. It thus becomes clear that whatever experience is, it is not, for Hume, identical with the *present* testimony of the senses; that can be only a cross-section of experience. ("Present" has at least two meanings in Hume: present in time, in present time; present to us, presented.) Experience as such consists rather in an accumulation of sensory perceptions. These are bound together by resemblance. They must add up to a record that is formidable. Experience is accumulative (rather than cumulative, for reasons that will later emerge). It is a fund, a fund of evidence or testimony. Not mere quantitative increase but repetition and recurrence are its essence. You do not believe the sun will rise tomorrow because you saw it rise yesterday, but because that case of seeing belongs to an indefinitely large and continuing assemblage of cases. For Hume, and contrary to the proverb, seeing is *not* believing. Not visual perception (or any other kind) alone but experience promises that the sun will rise again. Just why experience should provide assurance— why the habits of expectation that we form should constitute evidence—remains, to Hume and others, a mystery.

The Humean conception is surprisingly close to that of Aristotle, despite differences. For Aristotle, experience is one level among several levels of awareness. The lowest level is sensation. Then comes memory. Then comes experience, which depends upon the recurrence of this or that memory. A low level of awareness is one which yields knowledge of a simple or primitive kind; a high level is one which yields superior and far-reaching knowledge. What we call experience is familiarity with individual cases, individual circumstances or occurrences. Experience does, indeed, seem to imply awareness of what is common to these cases. It is, in a genuine sense, acquaintance with similarities. As in Hume, it is an accumulation, a fund of similar perceptions, preserved by memory. But it stops right there. And right there also stops the parallelism of Aristotle and Hume. For Aristotle feels that there are higher as well as lower levels than experience. The higher are the levels of art and science—of meritorious making and theoretical understanding. Experience is practical and basically reliable. The physician who cures by recognizing similarities among cases, even if he lacks theoretical knowledge, may do an effective job, and in the long run perhaps a better practical job than the theoretically equipped man who discerns many more factors in particular situations—perhaps too many (and distracting) factors for practical effectiveness. Art and science involve not only the recognition of similarities (as experience does) but their expression or formulation as universals, a grasp of the principles underlying them. On the intrinsic cognitive limitations of what they call experience Hume and Aristotle agree. But just as Hume may be said to reject the proverb "seeing is believing," Aristotle may be said to reject that other proverb "Experience is the best teacher."

Locke emphasizes a distinction between "external" and "internal" experience. "Experience" means for him that avenue of activity in which the human understanding gathers materials for its knowledge. The generic form in which such activity is carried on is what Locke calls "perception." External perception is perception of the qualities we encounter in the world. Internal perception is the perception of perception, and of its kinds. One might perhaps be prompted to think that it is internal experience which is the richer, subtler notion. But not in Locke's version. On the contrary, it is external perception, the "outer" side of experience, that emerges as more provocative and exciting. Perception as Locke understands it is far more varied and complicated than it will become in Hume. For in Locke the qualities of the world are more varied and complicated: We can be properly said to perceive not only color, shape, or sound, but meaning, relation, and interconnection; not only space, motion, and action, but unity, power, and existence. In internal experience, on the other hand, we perceive the mechanics of the understanding, its "operations" or ways of perceiving, such as remembering and abstracting. What is notable about this view of experience is the remarkable range of its activity, perception.

For an approach which regards internal experience not merely as an activity but as a world to be discovered, we must go mainly to the medieval period. St. Augustine, Platonist that he is, is moved by the idea of light and illumination. The most brilliant light is that which shines within the soul, the light variously called the divine light or light of nature. In this light is revealed the world of "inner" experience. And in this world are to be found the sources of truth, and the aspirations, hopes, and moral convictions of man. It is the world in which the ultimate justification of scientific principles is to be found, alongside the testimony of duty and conscience. Inner experience is also the realm of mysticism, which seeks to understand, indeed to encounter, God in the light that he has provided. To the same light, as we know, early modern scientists appealed. A striking exemplar of the internal-external conception of experience is St. Bonaventura. When he looks at the world outside, he finds "the footprints of God in creation." When he looks within himself, he finds "the sweet odor of Christ." These blunt images, and the lack of fear with which they are set forth, represent an intensity and a type of "experiential" exploration not duplicated in the modern period.

In one form or another, the inner-outer contrast continues to flourish. But whether in Locke or Descartes, whether among the medievals or moderns, it is beset by theoretical confusion. This is not the place to discuss the problem. I merely note, as some others have, that "internal" and "external" can scarcely be spatial terms; soul or mind does not admit of an inside and an outside in the sense of a discoverable boundary. Nor does it help much to say that "internal" and "external" are metaphorical terms. Metaphor is inevitable in common speech, and as I believe, inevitable in philosophy, as well as desirable. But these particular metaphors resist integration with other concepts. They are so widely used, both in common and in philosophic language, that like "experience" itself they evade scrutiny. Never having been satisfactorily analyzed to their advantage, they encourage a certain kind of intuitionism. They are, as it were, unofficial categories. Yet they cannot actually function as categories, being neither sufficiently abstract nor sufficiently vivid. Basically, they reflect the dogmas of common sense.

We are ready to consider a major variation in the conception of experience. But in order to do so, we must first stand off from the types of approach we have framed for consideration thus far, and ask whether, in spite of their substantial differences from each other, they have significant characteristics in common. The answer is that they have.

First, all of the usages described conceive of experience as necessarily entailing consciousness or awareness. Experience thus becomes something essentially relating to "mental action" or passive sensing. The accumulation of sensory encounters; the recurrence of similarities; the appeal to observation; the world that shines by divine light; the world of phenomena—all are in some way related to mind. From this approach it is often only a short step to the so-called problem of whether I can ever get outside of my own experience. And this problem, which has become a problem by resting comfortably on the assumption that consciousness is mandatory for experience, in turn breeds its own insoluble puzzles. It is also a short step to the question whether what we should mean by "nature" is "experience."

Second, all of the approaches thus far considered think of experience in terms of knowledge. They make experience a form of knowledge or a means to knowledge. In this respect they all conceive of experience as at least in part a kind of evidence—for example, evidence of the universal beyond the particular, or evidence of the fact beyond the appearance, or evidence of the creator beyond the created, or evidence of qualities in the world, or evidence restricted to the data of a self's private world. Some of the approaches regard experience as the poorest kind of evidence; others, as

the best kind; still others, as the only kind. But the
paramount concern of all is with the cognitive orientation and value of experience. It is with the assertive
claims made by man, their claims of truth. It is with
the feelings, suspicions, perceptions of man in so far as
these can be justified as veracious.

The variation of viewpoint alluded to a moment
ago, the one that contrasts sharply with the positions
we have just described collectively, is that of Hegel.
Now in one sense Hegel himself reflects emphatically
the two overall tendencies common to the other views.
The basic framework of experience for him too is
consciousness, and for him too experience is necessarily
bound up with knowledge. But the scope of consciousness and the scope of knowledge in Hegel's outlook are
so broad, so comprehensive, that the similarity of orientation only makes the differences stand out the more.

For Hegel experience is the very pith of the way in
which human consciousness functions. It is not a level
or a tool or a kind of evidence, not a mirror of something other than itself. It is the pulse and the intricate
rhythm of man's life. It is that which weaves together
the forces of consciousness, such as reason, knowledge,
and freedom. Thus reason, for example, is not opposed
to or contrasted with experience but is developed in it.
Hegel calls experience "the dialectic process which
consciousness executes on itself." Many have taken a
somewhat wooden view of this dialectic. They have
tended to regard it only as a kind of formula whereby
contradictory ideas, negations, become reconciled. Or
they have thought of it as a key to history, whereby the

clash of social movements and doctrines generates the next step in the so-called progress of man. We should certainly not underemphasize these aspects of Hegel's dialectic. But stated only in these ways, they do not adequately uncover what Hegel calls "experience." For this purpose we have to translate the dialectical process of consciousness into somewhat broader terms.

Recall that for Hume experience implies *sameness*, the repetitive force stabilizing our cognitive outlook on the world. For Hegel, on the contrary, experience implies *novelty*. Experience or the movement of consciousness aims to encompass novelty but at the same time to resist it; it struggles to absorb the new into the old, to adapt the old to the new. If, as we have suggested, the Humean emphasis is on the accumulative, the Hegelian is on the cumulative. The accumulative is an increasing aggregate of elements. The cumulative is an ongoing outcome of what develops. Regardless of whether new complications of thought (negative factors, contradictory aspects in the ideas we hold) are good or bad, profitable or unprofitable, they are relentlessly engaged by consciousness. Consciousness is therefore continually split, detached from itself. It exploits what threatens its unity, strives to preserve that unity, and evolves a new unity. This is the outcome of an arduous progression. Conflict, resistance, integration are the stuff of experience. In the experiential process thought and passion both play a role. Consciousness continually unravels and disentangles ideas; it fastens and builds up, rises and falls, gains and loses. Resolution, however, is inevitable, and each experiential cycle ends, as it began, with novelty, but another kind of novelty, that of the unified idea. The perspective of consciousness is once more enlarged. Consciousness is clarified, purged of obstructions to its thinking. Yet it is always subject to the burden of the next phase in the process.

Experience, then, is the inherent cognitive adventure within social and individual life. In Hegelian terms, it could be said to be neither the best nor the worst teacher; it is the only possible one. For human conscious life is necessarily its own teacher. Of the viewpoints thus far identified, only the Hegelian is able to provide a plausible interpretation for the common usage which we illustrated by the statement "That is what dramatists have found important in human experience"—human experience meaning the human struggle to know the self and the world.

I have suggested that for Hegel the concept of experience also contributes meaning to the concepts of reason and freedom. Experience, as the struggle for clarification of consciousness, is a clarification of purpose. But reason is precisely the strategy of conscious purpose, and it becomes more dominant with the march of dialectic. Here we arrive at one basic condition for freedom. The free person is one whose outlook is in accordance with rational clarity and purpose, whose actions stem from governance of the self by the rule of reason, in contrast to self-indulgence, exemption from principle, or exemption from compulsion.

Neither Hegel nor anyone else could say that for

individual selves the course of experience is necessarily a course of "progress." It is rather what we have called a progression, a moving onward, wherever the chips may fall. Individual consciousness is not always actually a movement toward the clearer or the better. But for Hegel it is in *human* consciousness that progress is to be found, whatever individual or social forms it takes. Regardless of particular failures, it is not the human mind that fails. Weakness, impotence, and confusion contribute indirectly but ultimately to the advance of knowledge. Hegel's optimism reflects a metaphysical position that links the advance of human knowledge with the movement of Universal Reason in the universe.

Hegel's analysis of the complications of consciousness is an important contribution to the theory of experience, whatever our critical reaction to it may be. The foregoing account lays as much emphasis as possible on a conception of experience as a comprehensive process. But the dominant role of thought and ideation in Hegel results in a subordinate role for making and doing. Hegel's awareness of the latter aspects of human life is keen enough. But they are not conceptually recognized by him as fundamental constituents of the experiential process. If experience *is* to be interpreted as a process with the multifariousness that characterizes human life, it cannot be understood as having a single kind of goal. It cannot be understood primarily in terms of consciousness and knowledge, mind and truth. Nor can it so easily be granted a cosmic role. Paradoxically, experience in Hegel is broadened by being linked to a cosmic process. Yet it is narrowed by being limited to only one side of the human process.

The most extensive and detailed treatment of the concept of experience in the history of western philosophy is that of John Dewey. But before turning to him, it makes sense to dwell briefly on a conception that is to be found in the writings of Charles Peirce. (I say "a" conception because there are several.) For Peirce experience is still a kind of consciousness, and actually a much more restricted kind than it is in Hegel. It has a very specific character. To cite Peirce's own illustration: "A whistling locomotive passes at high speed close beside me. As it passes the note of the whistle is suddenly lowered . . . I perceive the whistle . . . But I cannot be said to have a sensation of the change of note . . . the cognition of the change is of a more intellectual kind. That I experience rather than perceive." If I can be said to perceive qualities, then what I experience are events. Experience is the element of shock in consciousness. It is a "forcible modification of our ways of thinking." (Why, we may ask as we did of Hegel, modification only of our ways of *thinking*? Why not, more generally, of our *ways*, our ways of living, acting, making, relating?) It is a compulsive imposition upon us, emanating from the "world of fact," something we resist. Thus in experience proper (as distinct from perception) there is always a two-sidedness, in the sense of a duality, an opposition. It is not as it is in Hegel—something to be ideationally resolved. It is, on the contrary, brute and irreducible. Though it admits of degrees, the aspect of resistance and limited control is never eliminated.

We can see what is implied by this conception of experience. The human creature, on the one hand habit-ridden, and on the other hand subject to shocks making for change, is pre-eminently the learning creature. He is obliged to anticipate as well as to remember. He must make conjectures about the future as well as accumulate lessons from the past. And there are different methods that he can use to cushion the impact made upon him by the world. Science, Peirce believes, is the most dispassionate method of conjecturing. It respects but does not fear the compulsion of experience. Experience convinces us of what is the case, what are the facts. In this sense we can speak of "appealing" to experience. Pure science appeals to it only for the truths it can yield. Applied science uses these truths to anticipate the shocks of existence.

When I said that Dewey's reflections on the notion of experience are the most elaborate that we have, I did not mean to imply that they are made of one whole cloth. On the contrary, they are not always easy to fit together. Dewey combines a Hegelian-type emphasis on the continuity and movement of consciousness with a Peircean-type emphasis on thought's response to what is recalcitrant. But this amounts to a relatively small part of his viewpoint. In the broadest sense he sees experience as a kind of relation. It is a relation between a human organism and that part of the world which is said to constitute this organism's environment. There are many forms of environment, and within each form there are many situations or problematic areas. The organism moves from environment to environment, from problem to problem. Dewey likes to think of the experiential relation in these mobile terms. One of his main themes is what he sometimes calls "transaction," or "interaction" between organism and environment, meaning to affirm not simply that the organism is altered by the world but that alteration is mutual. Within this broad framework Dewey makes a number of distinctions. Thus, there is "experienc*ing*" and there are "experienc*es*." Among these experiences, most of which are routine and commonplace, there may emerge a significant instance which Dewey calls "*an* experience." There are two main levels of experience: primary or gross experience and secondary or "reflective" experience. And there are two main dimensions of experience: doing and undergoing.

Like Hegel, Dewey is impressed by the role of novelty. "Experience means the *new*, that which calls us away from adherence to the past, that which reveals novel facts and truths." But in contrast to Hegel, he introduces biological and social strains. Sooner or later, it also becomes clear why, in Deweyan terms, "learning from experience" has to mean "learning from experiment." Experience is not opposed to behavior; it includes behavior. Nor is experience opposed to knowledge; it includes knowledge (knowing). Dewey's contemporary, G. H. Mead, actually sees experience as constituted primarily by social behavior, that within which communication is embedded. Both Dewey and Mead, partly reflecting Hegel, find experience to be cyclical. The cycle they find, however, is one of alternating frustration and adjustment. Mead, laying emphasis on other organisms as a fundamental part of the environment, thinks of communication as that which produces both releasing and inhibiting action.

What for Hegel is the experiential struggle of thought with its own depths and internal oppositions, is for Dewey and Mead the experiential process of problem-solving. Whereas for Hegel the focus of experience is the Idea, for Dewey it is the situation. The reconciliation of conflicting traits of thought becomes the concern with conflicting or unresolved situations. The life of consciousness is transformed into, or enlarged to become, the life of the human animal, an animal laden with problems and searching for intrinsic satisfactions. It is not hard to see why Dewey early laid stress on the philosophic significance of Darwinism. Darwin roused him from his dogmatic slumbers and led him to regard man as the problem-solving animal. Problem-solving, he believes, permeates everyday life and is central to artistic no less than to scientific endeavor. It does not mean that action is the only factor in experience, nor does action in turn mean merely movement in space or pushing and pulling. Similarly, what Dewey regards as an environment need not take the form of a set of physical circumstances in present time. An environment, he points out, might emerge from a book a person is reading, so that the environing conditions would be, say, "England or ancient Greece or an imaginary region."

Dewey's two experiential dimensions, doing and undergoing, represent his version of the traditional contrast between activity and passivity. Sometimes he renders them in the form of a distinction between instrumental and consummatory experience. This is a distinction between experience as seeking means and experience as attaining ends. When an individual achieves a balance between doing and undergoing, then, says Dewey, he may be said to have *an* experience ("an integral event"), a whole which is "complete in itself." In *an* experience there is a genuine beginning, middle, and ending, but the whole is what Dewey calls a unitary quality within experienc*ing*. The conception of *an* experience is closely connected with Dewey's conception of "aesthetic" experience.

Consider once again the general structure of Dewey's position. Experience in the broadest sense is experiencing. It is the natural relation of interaction with an environment, a relation which in its changing aspects takes the form of a process. Within this process the individual copes with problems. Through doing and undergoing he tries to solve or resolve these problems, to turn unclear and unpredictable situations into manageable ones. These are among his experiences. Now and then there is *an* experience in which various unorganized details are organized into a wholeness, a meaningful specimen of value.

Dewey's concern with the importance of the concept of experience has provoked distortion of his general philosophic position. He has been criticized for confounding nature with experience, for laying too much emphasis on "the foreground" (Santayana). Or, it has been said, Dewey has so magnified experience that it has become a domain which has crowded out nature and diminished its metaphysical importance.

The injustice of this criticism is patent. Those who authored it were attributing to Dewey a conceptual model of experience which they had inherited, and which Dewey's use of the *term* "experience" resuscitated for them, thereby overshadowing the actual substance of his position. Their model, hopelessly linked with the term, was that of experience as enclosing the self, derived (and understandably) from the net effect upon them of Berkeley, Kant, and Hegel. That Dewey, in enlarging the notion of experience, was not perpetuating but trying relentlessly to undermine this model was what they could not see. Dominated by the established classifications of philosophic doctrine, they focussed more on the familiar-sounding locutions Dewey used than on the meanings which his context determined. No matter how often he insisted that experience is one manifestation of nature; that experience is precisely the name for the relation in which nature and human nature are joined; that experience is literally man's natural mode of existence; the charges of subjectivism and anthropocentrism continued to be made. For some of the misunderstandings Dewey himself was partly responsible. His lack of inventiveness in terminology and his excessively informal metaphysical structure gave opportunity to the uncharitable.

And yet there are genuine difficulties in Dewey's

position. Some of them indicate that his conception of experience is not free from limiting and restricting elements native to the tradition we have been tracing. As he sees doing and undergoing, there must be (should be?) in individual experience a kind of balance or harmony, a unified equilibrium of the two aspects. Otherwise we do not have *an* experience. Just *what* kind of balance is required; indeed, just what constitutes a "balance" in this regard, and what determines an "integral" event, is not made clear. Why any event experienced is not integral in its own way, *as* an event, is also not made clear. It would seem that an experience acquires its distinctive unity in virtue of some kind of feeling or felt quality. But this does not help to clarify, since Dewey regards "qualities" as "indescribable" and "indefinable." But aside from "an" experience, for Dewey the process of experiencing as such requires the individual to be an agent who consciously perceives and anticipates. From this requirement it follows that any individual whom events affect, but without his agency, his awareness, his assent or dissent, his choice or intention, is somehow excluded from an experience and from experiencing. If this is what the concept of experience entails, then clearly another concept is required to fill the explanatory gaps. Dewey seems to lay more emphasis on a certain kind of packaging by the individual than on what is relevant to the individual's continuing course of life. Moral and aesthetic considerations seem to take precedence over metaphysical coherence and adequacy. Are not the effects of disease or social disaster, however gradual and imperceptible they may be, of as much importance to an individual as anything he would initiate? The consequences he endures are still consequences whether they stem from his direct action and perception or from any other circumstance. Actually they may effect the deepest transformation of his subsequent experience. For after all, it is his being that has been modified, now and in the future, and what is most fundamental for him is the character of the modification.

Two basic features of Dewey's viewpoint thus emerge: (1) What happens to an individual cannot be part of his experience unless it stems from his own action. (2) What happens to an individual cannot be part of his experience unless he is aware of it. These two features are present both early and late in Dewey's thinking, and they show that traditional ideas die hard, even in a philosopher of Dewey's stature. "To have an experience," he says, "the action and its consequence must be joined in perception." But are the sufferings of Job and Hamlet not part of their "experience"? The travail they undergo does not for the most part conform to Dewey's requirement; it does not "perceptibly result from what [they] had done." Dewey's strong concern with the ethical, social, and aesthetic aspects of man's being—otherwise admirable —is what leads him to overemphasize purpose, awareness, direct action, and anticipated consequences. It helps to explain his frequent jumbling of metaphysical and moral issues—a fault he often ascribes to the Greek philosophers. He confuses the traits of experience with the traits of morally important experience.

It seems clear that human experience can develop and individual experience can be modified whether, in any given instance, there is agency without awareness, awareness without agency, or neither of the two elements. Do the discordant strains in Dewey's theory indicate that the very concept "experience" is worn thin and will not tolerate any more distinctions or mendings? I am myself persuaded that, from a philosophic point of view, the concept is functionally spent. But then, our philosophic obligation is not to close up shop; it is to develop a fresher group of concepts that preserves what is worth preserving in the old and that accomplishes what the old has failed to accomplish. In terms of such a possible new start, let us examine a certain aspect of Dewey's theory.

Is the line between doing and undergoing so sharp that we can say confidently what is initiatory action and what is not? Or what an individual can undergo without doing and do without undergoing? Such questions have theoretical importance for an adequate metaphysics of the human process. Here I can only indicate what are the inadequacies of Dewey's twin concept. Doing and undergoing are regarded by Dewey as separable and independently variable. An individual may do much and undergo little, or undergo much and do little. Strictly, it would seem that he may neither do nor undergo, for instance when he is asleep, and this in turn would seem to imply that the course of his experience may be discontinuous. Yet a phrase like "in all my experience" seems to demand an interpretation of experience as continuous in some basic sense, as does the phrase "the course of experience." Dewey has not integrated experiencing and experiences.

The conception of doing or acting is linked by Dewey to the primacy of the means-end process. It is a too-limited conception. Doing seems to mean designing and executing. Not that Dewey wishes to deny automatic or involuntary behavior. But we are speaking of experience, and of doing as a dimension of experience. To think of doing as necessarily instrumental is an oversimplification. We need to recognize non-instrumental and non-problematical doing. Important as problematical experience may be, it is not the primary character of experiencing, and actually not the whole of the dimension of action. Not even all *methodic* activity is an attempt to solve problems. Dewey believes that art and science alike exemplify problem-solving. But if an artist *may* be engaged in problem-solving of one sort or another within his work, he also may *not*. His methodic experience may be that of shaping materials through the cultivation of his powers and propensities. The completion of his product, as I have stated elsewhere, may "wait upon the mere passage of time, or upon the occurrence of an inclination, or upon eventual growth in perception. A task to be accomplished is not the same as a problem to be solved."

Turning to the Deweyan category of undergoing, the reason that it too is narrowly construed is that it is limited to conscious response. Dewey thinks of it mainly as affective or sensory awareness. What of the unnoticed habits that human beings acquire; the unperceived unappreciated trends of thinking that they nevertheless absorb and transmit; the hidden and disguised attitudes they grow into; the feeling-tendencies that are theirs without their awareness? These are surely fundamental to experience. And what, moreover, of the fact that when human beings do feel and know that they feel, they may not feel anything as yet articulated; what of the fact that their fear or joy may be generalized or diffused? Dewey's analysis, we may add, is not adapted to recognize randomness, perversity, and waste in human experience as authentic constituents. A sanguine streak, for which a philosopher normally may be forgiven or even commended, crops up periodically to mar his generalizations.

In this introduction to the chapter that follows I have not inquired directly into the implications which non-philosophic thought may have for a philosophic theory of experience. I have assumed, however, as this book and its successors do, that an adequate philosophic conception should be able to encompass aspects of human life reflected by the sciences and arts, by moral and religious attitudes, and by what takes place psychologically, socially, technologically.

Among the philosophic orientations that I have not considered here, there are some (James, Whitehead) for which experience is, at least in principle, intended not to be limited to man, nor even to living creatures. In another work I have described a version of such a view as holding that experience "overflows the bounds of human life and becomes virtually synonymous with relatedness of any kind among [actual] things of any kind." And in commenting upon this, I go on to say: "the ironic consequence is that, though experience is construed as escaping the confines of mind, it does so in a dubious sense, because the categories of mind themselves, as it turns out, have been extended to the whole of nature."

Whitehead has said, "The word 'experience' is one of the most deceitful in philosophy." He himself, no doubt for good reason, clings to the use of the word. And we too, though less reliant on it, will keep it in the wings, with the hope that fewer and sharper appearances will heighten the value of its role.

TOWARD A GENERAL THEORY OF
HUMAN JUDGMENT

I
PROCEPTION

To ASK whether the human individual is best understood as a multiplicity or as a unity is unprofitable, not because the answer is impossible but because the answer is obvious. The humanity of the individual implies a plurality of functions, and the individuality of the man implies a focus of movement and of utterance. The notion of the integral individual, as a frame of reference by which specific acts and patterns can be better understood, is not new but has rather found a renascence of favor in philosophy, psychology, and medicine. Yet an idea with so acceptable a ring has remained singularly undeveloped so far as philosophic categorization is concerned. The tools of interpretation continue to be such concepts as "self," "character," "organism," and "personality." These concepts, each of which in its own way and in its varied contexts enables us to understand and categorize many phenomena, are not to be depreciated. It is not their serviceability that is to be questioned but their metaphysical adequacy, their comprehensiveness. They are especially deficient as vehicles of a philosophy of communication, method, and reason; and although it is not within the province of this book primarily to establish this contention, perhaps the succeeding chapters can serve as indirect evidence.

If the view that individuality implies unity has any meaning at all, it means that the individual functions in a unitary way, that each activity or each mode of activity is a phase of a single process. The expression "functions in a unitary way" is circumlocutory and less than illuminating; yet there seem to be no available categories by which it is possible to do better, even thus in a mere allusion to the rudimentary human process. Is this process, for instance, adequately designated by the terms "experience" and "experiencing"? It should be no longer necessary to detail the numerous ambiguities that such terms breed. Even when, by a great and vigorous stroke, their narrowing mentalistic overtones are expelled, questionable philosophic associations linger or enter insidiously. And even when the terms are limited arbitrarily, to signify, for example, the interaction of the individual with an environment, we are told little about the status and meaning of individuality. Equally and perhaps more evidently unsatisfactory are the terms "behavior" and "behaving," which are too narrow and excessively physiological or psychological in import. Paradoxically, "experiencing" is not broad enough to include all forms of behavior, and "behaving" is not broad enough to include all phases of experience.

The interplay of the human individual's activities and dimensions, their unitary direction, constitutes a process which I shall call *proception*. The term is designed to suggest a moving union of seeking and receiving, of forward propulsion and patient absorption. Proception is the composite, directed activity of the individual. Any instance of his functioning, any event in his history enters into the proceptive direction. Reciprocally, and perhaps more significantly, the way that an individual will act at any time, and the way in which his intellectual and moral character will be modified, depends on his proceptive direction. Proception is the process in which a man's whole self is summed up or represented. On this idea that the whole individual is the cumulative representative of the moving individual I should like to lay the major stress. To say that the human animal is a proceiving animal is to state the most general or pervasive attribute of his being, and at the same time the most distinctive attribute. The theory of the distinctive human activities, such as imagination and creation,* should become more intelligible when these are seen as properties of the proceiver rather than as properties of the thinker or feeler. It could be said that these are functions of the man and not of the mind, if this aphoristic form of expression could manage to convey the suggestion of directed, integral movement. It is the proceiver, then, not a physiological or intellectual capacity of the proceiver, that wonders, asserts, interrogates. These are proceptive functions. Traveling, hearing, and eating are certainly relevant to proception, but they are not generic in the sense that they can characterize the proceptive direction. So far as the nature of the individual influences the nature of the individual's world, it can be said that the hearing apparatus determines what is heard, but that the proceptive direction determines the quality of conscience and the image of gods, the demand for harmonious satisfaction and the tolerance of possibilities, the hunger of eros and of reason and of art.

* For further clarification of this term, please see Appendix.

The content of the summed-up-self-in-process, the individual's world, is the proceptive domain. The proceptive domain of an individual is a part of the world and the whole of a self uniquely represented. By nature man proceives—he moves as an accumulating whole. What changes within a man, and varies from man to man, is the specific character of the proceptive domain. Within the process of proception the character of the proceptive domain may alter in kind and in degree, and in an indefinite number of ways. The proceptive domain defines the relative largeness and scope of the self. How much of heaven and earth is part of the individual determines how much he is part of them. The proceptive process is the ongoing representation of the human aspect of the human animal. Spinoza, and Aristotle before him, held that the divine in a man is a function of his rational largeness. Rationality in its most fundamental sense is a property of the proceptive process; a property predicable of the proceptive domain but not of every proceptive domain.

An object* or situation falls within the proceptive domain if it is present to the individual in the sense of affecting or addressing his powers. I mean to use the phrase "present to" in a temporal as well as in a structural sense—though certainly not in the sense of being confined to the so-called immediate present—for it is his gross present possession and present direction that define or determine the individual. Of all the facts and situations that may be said to relate to an individual, some modify, some promote or reinforce, and some are irrelevant to his proceptive direction. An object or situ-

* For further clarification of this term, please see Appendix.

ation is present to an individual, is part of his proceptive domain—and when it is we shall call it a procept—
if it actually either modifies or reinforces his proceptive
direction. Some objects or facts, like the depth of a
crater on the moon, may be irrelevant to the character
of proception and hence fall outside the proceptive domain. To be a procept is not necessarily to be noticed,
felt, or attended to in awareness. An occupational
routine is as much a procept as a pain; past moral train-
ing as much as a momentary sense of obligation. But
far-off diplomatic intrigue may for a given individual
not be a procept. Ontologically, it may stand in some relation to him, but may not actually modify or reinforce
his proceptive direction. An active disease, the circulation of the blood, or the structure of the basic organs
may all be procepts, influencing the character of the individual as proceiver. A fly alighting on a sleeve is not
likely to be a procept; but a fly observed is a procept,
for it reinforces the habits of expectation and their
limits. An idea or practice accepted or adopted by an
individual is a procept: idea-accepted-by-X is a natural
complex characterizing an individual as proceiver.

The law of gravitation and the rotation of the earth
sustain a man's life and make possible the very fact
of his proceiving; yet they may or may not affect his
proceptive direction. For in the very same sense, and
indifferently, they affect every possible proceptive direction, and they sustain death as well as life. Not every
fact that is simply related to an individual is a procept.
The shape of the oesophagus may be proceptively negligible though somatically distinctive. A procept is any-

thing that is a property *of* the individual, that happens *to* him, that affects or characterizes him in any way at all, so long as it relates to him *as a proceiver* (as an identifiable and cumulative individual) and not as a mere entity in the cosmic maelstrom.

What particularly does or does not fall within a proceptive domain is theoretically determinable, not by simple inspection but by a difficult process of abstraction. I mean to affirm the precarious tenure of the self in the world and the indefinite boundaries of the self, not to contrast an inner and outer life or an inner and outer world. Procepts are not just objects or situations, natural complexes (though they are at least that), nor are they just "data" (though they are at least that, in a broad and non-psychologistic sense of the term); they are natural complexes in-active-relation-to a proceiver. The concepts of proceptive domain and proceptive direction make it possible to express the unity of the individual by emphasizing his continuity with himself, and the fluidity of the individual by emphasizing his continuity with the world.

Within the proceptive domain three perspectives* may be distinguished. The *gross* proceptive domain comprises all that belongs to the individual's living makeup, the segment of nature within which he functions, the past that is actually or potentially alive for him, the sum of his suppositions, guiding principles, commitments, and peculiarities. The gross domain is the class of all his interrelated procepts. The *floating* proceptive domain represents the summed-up self or proceiver within a given situation. The limits of a given situation or

---

* For further clarification of this term, please see Appendix.

enterprise are in the last analysis assignable by stipulation. Sometimes they may be defined by means of the formulation of a problem. But not every situation is a problematic situation. A situation for an individual is the concatenated set of interests, occupations, or problems that he would declare it to be if he were made articulate by a daemonic or Socratic gadfly. This does not imply that he cannot be in a situation which he is unaware of, or that he may not be·in various situations that simultaneously apply to him. An individual is in as many situations as there are viewpoints from which his proceptive direction can be described. The floating domain varies with each situation, or may be said to be the situation compositely determined by the indefinite class of overlapping situations. Finally, the *imminent* proceptive domain comprises all that is present to—that is, available for—the proceiver at a given moment; it is the gross domain represented in minimal cross section. (I use the term "imminent" rather than "immediate" because I wish to suggest the cross section of a process rather than merely of an existent whole; and because the term "immediate" carries certain epistemological implications which, as I shall explain later, I wish to avoid.) The imminent domain is not an "essence intuited" or an "image of self" that a man carries about in his head; it is the world of the self in abstraction from the self's past and future. It is the directly available upshot of the whole of the individual's proception. It is what an ideal biography would reveal his self to be at a given moment if his life were arrested at that moment. I should like to emphasize that "procept" and "present to" have been so defined as to render non-sensical such statements as "Procept A is more truly present than procept B," or "Procepts in the imminent domain are more truly present than procepts in the floating domain," or "This procept is present to the imminent domain but not to the floating or gross domains."

I have called the three domains perspectival distinctions. Perspectives are no less "real" or identifiable than individuals. To subdivide the proceptive domain perspectivally is important if only as a new recognition of the old truth that the notion of unity goes hand in hand with the notions of plurality and diversity. From the definition of "proception" it is seen to be a metaphysical fact that there is one proceptive direction for what we ordinarily call and wish to call an "individual." But the qualitative complexity inherent in this direction may be expressed as greater or less in proportion as the floating domain makes it possible to understand or generalize about the gross domain. The less reliable the imminent domain is as a sample of the floating domain, or the floating domain as a sample of the gross domain, the more complex (in the sense of qualitatively plural) the proceptive direction. "Complexity" is a term which is morally neutral and systematically ambiguous.*

Now in the expression "the individual proceives" the verb is used intransitively: "proceives" has properly no namable entity as object. A man imagines his next purchase or topic of a discussion; he remembers a hurricane or a nightmare; he perceives the dawn or the hostility of his neighbor. But he proceives* nothing less than

* For further clarification of this term, please see Appendix.

his world, and nothing in particular. He functions in a
universally available world individually appropriated.
In whatever specific way he acts or functions, he proceives. The soul may not always think, but the man always proceives. A procept is not "designated"; it is not
a "referent"; it is not an "object" of proception in the
sense that the latter is an intending act. It is not something that has a fixed prior integrity or pre-ordained
organization. A procept is whatever natural complex
can be identified or discriminated in the life process
of the individual. An object is one and the same for
any number of individuals; a procept, by definition, is
that object as uniquely standing in relation to a given
individual.

Modern philosophy has asked certain kinds of questions and has made certain kinds of distinction which
on the surface may appear germane to the concept of
proception. It has asked how data enter experience,
what the given is, whether percepts are simple or complex, whether ideas, essences, or sensa mediate between
the individual and the world, and whether experience
screens us off from nature. Hovering behind these questions and their conditioned answers is a vacillation between the conception of experience as the given and
experience as the funded. This distinction stems mainly
from an empiricist tradition concerned with "data"
and presentations. From another tradition, going back
at least to St. Augustine, there stems the preoccupa-
tion with the given of internal experience apprehended
by internal observation. Experience is equated with a
continuous life of total awareness; but along with this,

as a kind of analogue to funded experience, has come the beloved fund of *a priori* insights and judgments. Recent conceptions of experience in terms of shock or struggle or interaction and transaction have served as antidotes to the earlier conceptions, although recent literature and the climate of contemporary discussion witness the fact that they have not escaped with entire success from the epistemological morass. I am not here concerned to examine the effectiveness of these opinions. But it is necessary, for the purpose of amplification, to deal briefly with certain types of questions that might be raised in the traditional epistemological manner and that might erroneously be considered problems for the present approach. Thus it might conceivably be asked how procepts "enter" the proceptive domain, what the relation is between procepts and "the given," whether procepts are "simple or complex," whether the procept or the proceptive domain "mediates" between the individual and the world, and whether an individual can "get outside of" his proceptive domain. I cannot assume that such questions should be seen to be irrelevant or to be obviated at their face value.

It may be a genuine problem to ask whether or how a "sense datum" or an "essence" or an abstract idea can "fall within" a "field of consciousness." Or it may be a problem (of a far more significant character) to ask how an abstract idea can enter into communication, when, for instance, a purely behavioristic explanation is attempted. But it is not a problem to ask how a procept can become part of a proceptive domain— that is, no more of a problem than how a citizen can become part of a nation, how a man can fall in love, how a color can enter the field of vision, or how a geographical area can be part of a climatic zone. The situation is one that calls for descriptive elaboration, not for linguistic reform or the dissolution of a paradox. The terms "procept" and "part of a proceptive domain" are synonymous; so that the question under consideration, to avoid tautology, must become: How does an event, object, or situation become a procept? But facts relate to the individual through some specific activity, and the "how" must here be addressed to the historian and psychologist whose task it is to investigate different levels of activity in a proceiver or in his society.

Procepts can be *either* "simple" *or* "complex," depending on how we choose to understand these terms. Some elements of the proceptive domain are fleeting, some enduring; some elusive, others compelling; some within the pale of awareness, others not. In so far as each of these procepts is qualitatively or ontologically an integrity, all are equally simple. Each affects the proceiver in just the way it does, and in this sense is irreducible and indivisible. But in its concrete history and ontological status every procept has an indefinite number of relations, dimensions, and constituents; and in this sense all are complex. As objects of inquiry all procepts are analyzable. Anything at all that affects the proceptive process can theoretically be described and explained in terms of the conditions under which it did so and in terms of the indefinite number of ramifications which it has. These ramifications and potential relations are as much "part" of the procept as are elements in its qualitative constitution. The relational status of procepts makes it impossible to conceive of them as entitative lumps geometrically divisible.

Must the "given," then, be denied? To the individual, however the concept of individuality be developed, there is unquestionably something "given" in some sense at all times. There is no reason why the notion of the given should not be usefully generalized. The traditional error in philosophies of the given is narrowness—even arbitrary narrowness—in the conception of what it is that is given. For the fundamental proceptive movement of the individual anything that contributes to, anything that influences the formation of the "self" or its habituation, is a "datum." From this point of view, every procept is given. Nothing is more or less given: bronchitis and cruel disposition no less than red patches seen and clanging bells heard. If the given is the available, then it is identical with the proceptive domain. A plausible identification seems to suggest itself—of the given with the imminent proceptive domain. But a number of distinctions and qualifications would need to be made at the outset. First, we have agreed that such a procept as the persistent action of the social heritage is as much given as a momentary sensation, and we ought not to lapse into the confusion of the traditional type of distinction; both procepts are available, and if either of the two can be said to be "available" in a dubious sense it is the sensation, which is both elusive and refractory. Second, we must not confuse the imminent domain with a "realm of immediacy." The imminent domain is not the "foreground" and the gross domain the "background" of proception. The one is a reflection of the other at a given moment. What is "available" in the one is available in the other, but the context is narrower. The role which a procept plays in the gross domain may not be determinable from the perspective of that same procept in the imminent domain. The given, then, is equally given, whether it be regarded as a whole or as arrested at a proceptive point.

Is the complex of my domestic, economic, and social status a result of inferential reconstruction, or a result of "construction," whereas the color of the page before me is "given"? The former is far more fundamental in my life, and more pervasive and compelling in my total awareness. In the proceptive domain of the mystic, the "evidence of things unseen" is as much given as that of things seen, and far more vividly enjoyed. Groundless presumption in the mystic occurs only when to these procepts—which like all procepts are natural complexes in a unique relation—a special cognitive significance is attached, and when from them a cognitive leap is made. The evidence of things unseen is here not evidence at all but proceptive presence, subject to further interpretation.

The proceptive domain is not something that "mediates" or "intervenes" between the individual and the world. The traditional question whether an individual can "get outside" or "reach beyond" or "transcend" his experience, or whether he is "shut off" or "enveloped" by appearances, may not be futile in terms of the traditional conceptual framework but it certainly is irrelevant to the present approach. In one sense a man is indeed enveloped in experience that may properly be called his own; it is not that all experience is a part of him but that *his* experience is a part of him, and he can no more get "outside" it than he can become another individual or become liberated from all perspective. The concepts we have introduced eliminate the ambiguities that nourish the "problem." To ask whether the individual can "intend" or "mean" or "refer to" anything outside his proceptive domain is as pointless as to ask whether he can escape from his proceptive domain: whether he can cease to be himself. This is not to deny that there is a sense in which the individual can be said to transcend himself, for instance, in his identification with a community. This identification is itself a procept, and the proceptive domain has simply been modified, however great the cultural or moral implication involved; "transcendence" here suggests the relative degree of novelty by which the individual's direction has been altered, or the relative extent of the reversal in direction which has taken place. If an individual cannot utterly cease to be himself, his proceptive direction can be profoundly altered. So that, if he must be regarded as insulated by his proceptive domain, this can mean in the last analysis only that he is not omnipotent or omnivorous. The individuality of the individual, his finitude, is his limitation to the dominant perspective in his life. Proception is the basic relationship in which a man stands to the world. (There could be little meaning in speaking of the basic relationship in which the world stands to him.) A segment of the

world is perforce the matter of his proception; his proception is a fact of the world.

There are two fundamental and correlative dimensions* in the proceptive direction: manipulation and
assimilation. Manipulation is not to be identified with
adjustment; it is by far the broader term, and much
in human activity that can be seen as manipulation
could not without strain and even absurdity be called
adjustment. On the latter notion recent thinking has
laid considerable and even exaggerated emphasis, so
that, for instance, it has been said of an activity like
imagination that "the conscious adjustment of the new
and the old *is* imagination."[1] There is a great and understandable attractiveness in the view which would
find adjustment, accommodation, and adaptation the
principal human dimensions. It is strengthened by the
indubitable continuity of man with lower biological
forms, and it gives the appearance of being strengthened
by a corollary that can easily spring from this consideration, namely, that man is essentially a problem-
solving animal. Unquestionably, the greater part of a
man's life is passed under the relentless pressure to conquer, and he never can escape the general problem of
stabilization, whether temperamental or environmental.
Whether problem-solving and adjustment are synonymous is in itself very much open to question. In any
case, neither concept is adequate for the analysis of
proception.

In the process of imagination we may explore the
new without consciously comparing it with the old,
and we may compare the new and the old without

* For further clarification of this term, please see Appendix.

consciously seeking to adjust the one to the other. Exploration and comparison, which are manipulative, may at least without contradiction be called non-adjustive. And in imagination the new may also be accepted for what it is, independently of manipulation. Its structural, qualitative being may enter the proceptive domain in non-instrumental awareness and be accepted, whether pleasurably or painfully, voluntarily or involuntarily. But the assimilative dimension of man does not necessarily entail awareness. Habituation, for instance, is a process of endurance as well as of formation. We assimilate not just sensible qualities, but advancing age, changing modes of thought, and the ethical temper of society. In a literal sense we may speak of manipulation and assimilation as essential attributes of proception. The most rudimentary facts of human living are the gross motion of continuance and the gross acceptance of a world.

In the manipulative dimension of his being, the individual is the actor, the agent, as in the assimilative he is the spectator, sufferer, patient; and he is both actor and spectator literally and inevitably. Suppose a man struggling to escape from a house on fire. Animal sagacity, panic, and practical inference are juxtaposed in a situation big with adjustive manipulation. Yet the entire situation is an enduring contemplative pattern, in each moment of which there is represented an independent contemplative pattern. A door appears through the smoke. It is a sign of possible passage. But it also is what it is, that sign and no other, making possible the adaptive inference of escape by impressing

its qualitative integrity upon attention. The instantaneous spectacle of the door is accepted qua spectacle,
and in so far, disinterestedly. In the natural and justi-
fiable contrast between theory and experiment, the
former, when regarded in a broad sense as an attribute
of imagination, has been identified with the spectatorial aspect of understanding, the latter with the manipulative. Certain pragmatists, of course, have recognized the manipulative character of theory. It is equally
essential to recognize in experiment the factor of contemplative acceptance. Each moment or stage of
experimental activity offers itself inevitably for assimilation, as does the whole of the formally envisioned and
manipulated enterprise.

In justifying the co-dimensionality and irreducibility
of assimilation we must avoid the suggestion that it
boils down ultimately to a succession of moments each
dumbly intuitive. For like manipulation, assimilation
occurs in physiological striving as well as in abstract
imagination, and in social movement as well as mental.
Every situation is pervaded with a spectatorial aspect.
The spectatorial has been too often identified with the
visual, the intellectually as well as the optically visual.
Whether it be attached to an overpowering emotional
state or to a dispassionate parade of associations, to kinaesthetic inertia or to a selection of prospects and possibilities; whether it characterize an individual of great
or small capacity, the spectatorial bent resides neu-
trally, as it were, within the proceptive direction. The
solver of a problem is also the acceptor of what it involves, an acceptance imposed by the pressure of the

world of which he is part and sustained by him with
the elemental patience requisite for life. The man in
the fire, wholly preoccupied within a situation of potential disaster, does not just glimpse the pattern of
this door and that column of smoke; one dimension of
his being is doomed by nature to bear witness to the
being of the whole.

I have ascribed assimilation to physiological striving
as well as to imagination. How, it may be asked, can
the physiological man be a spectator? The question
assumes an analysis of the individual in terms of a
collection of activities to only one or another of which
the spectatorial function is attributed. In one influential tradition, still very much alive, the mind is the
passive spectator, the body the active manipulator; and
thus biologistic theories of experience might understandably frown on the very idea of a spectator. But the
individual as spectator is the individual actor, one and
the same proceiver. Assimilation is not intellectual ac-
quiescence or intuitive ratification. Not by sensing or
by knowing does the individual become the spectator,
but by responding to the sheer presence of his procepts.
"Bearing witness" is perhaps excessively metaphorical.
Assimilation is proceptive toleration.

But the procciver is not simply "both" a manipulator and an assimilator, in the sense, for instance, that
he is "both" a walker and an eater. In manipulating
he is also assimilating; in assimilating, he is also manipulating. Thus in the simple act of seeing there is a
maneuvering of eye and position, and correlatively
there is an acceptance of a framework within which

eye and object are located as well as of the properties
envisioned. The activities of respiration and circulation
involve manipulation and assimilation. To be sure, it
is not the lungs and the blood vessels which do the
manipulating and assimilating, at least in the sense of
which I am speaking. It is the proceiver, in the perpetuation of his metabolic functions and in the inevitable selection of his environmental situations. Like
proception itself, the dimensions of proception do not
admit of any contrary except death. The individual
may not accept in the moral sense of the term, but
proceptively he assimilates all things as they are, that
is, as they are for him. Although the two dimensions
are ontologically inseparable, it may be advantageous to
emphasize or to abstract one or another within a given
perspective of analysis. This would mean that one or
the other dimension *is* primary *in* a given respect. Thus
we might try to understand the activity of art by emphasizing in it the aim of deliberative assimilation, and
the activity of science by emphasizing in it the quest
for the power of manipulation. With this it would not
be incompatible to emphasize, in some other perspective, the manipulative element in art and the assimilative element in science.

The concept of a proceptive *direction* must avoid
two misconceptions. One is that the movement of the
proceiver as proceiver implies teleological ordering by
some master plan of nature or of deity. Such an implication is no more justifiably inferable from the facts
of proception than from the other facts of nature; the
argument of Hume's *Dialogues* applies indifferently.

The second misconception is that every manifestation of proceptive activity involves a means-end relationship, or that a specific purpose inheres in each situation. I have already suggested that assimilation can be non-instrumental and is so for the most part. But there is an even deeper-lying basis of the non-instrumental in man. All of proception is characterized by a strain of ineradicable randomness, which might almost be regarded as a third proceptive dimension. Eyes function and see nothing in particular, bodies struggle but with no antagonist. A residuum of irrelevancy, of superfluity and waste of life is an ingredient in the human process. The individual, besides reconciling himself to and assimilating the world, abides with himself and the world in aimless passivity. Sheer drift is ubiquitous and undramatic, but it often translates itself into one or another form of sensibility.

The idea of a proceptive direction may perplex those who, finding it useful, nevertheless feel common parlance to be correct in saying that *some* individuals "lack direction." The term, it must be confessed, lends itself easily to misinterpretation. It seems to carry the flavor of a harmonious, coordinated purposiveness in the life of the individual. If used in this sense, phenomena like the dispersion and division of personality would make it a matter of specific factual inquiry to determine whether or not "direction" is present in a given individual. But proceptive direction has nothing to do with direction in this sense. The latter is predicable of certain individuals, the former of any individual. Proceptive direction concerns the potential course and outcome of what at any moment is the net manifold effect of an individual's history. Conflict, psychosis, and physical decomposition, before they destroy, yield a multiple integrity.

In an adequate theory of human utterance, the concept of proception would not eliminate the concept of experience. No amount of legislation will expel the term "experience" from common discourse or philosophic speculation, and perhaps this is just as well. The generality, as well as the vagueness, of the term answers and stems from the ever-present need for a way of designating a number of metaphysically discriminable situations that are somehow felt to be related: the effect upon individuals of factors in nature that do not seem to be identified or identifiable with them; the qualitative characters of this effect; the relative persistence of this effect in the make-up of individuals; and the interindividual fabric that seems at once to transcend the limits of an individual and yet to be available to that individual. Various philosophic traditions have magnified or exaggerated one and another aspect of this complex, and the result has of course been the erection of incompatible metaphysical structures. The concept of proception facilitates a juster theory of experience by supplying the means for interpreting it in multidimensional terms.

When experience is interpreted in terms of felt immediacy, certain inevitable philosophic problems and presuppositions crop up, some of which are suggestive and important, but some of which, on the other hand, are stultifying and futile. Now, uninterpreted feeling is a property that can belong to any phase of proception. It is no more a property of the imminent than of the floating proceptive domain. Among the procepts that dominate the elemental routine of animal living, sensory qualities appear to occupy a prominent place. From this fact it is a short and tempting step to the generalization that the "immediate" is what is somehow "closer" to the individual, to the "conscious subject." The next step that recommends itself is to ask the question whether that which is closer is somehow cognitively more authoritative or reliable or fundamental. But the theory of proception requires a very different approach to the issue of "closeness" than does the pseudospatial notion of immediate experience. The threefold subdivision of the proceptive domain may appear, instead, to follow equally misleading temporal lines. But that they follow such lines is only partly, and not essentially, the case. We have spoken of the imminent domain as the proceiver at a given moment, or as the ultimate cross section of the gross domain. The distinction is, however, primarily in contextual or situational terms. The gross domain is the ramified order within which any situation of the individual is discernible; the floating domain comprehends any such situation; and the imminent domain comprehends the minimal context of any such situation—or better, *any* minimal context of any situation. The minimal situation happens also to be the temporal minimum for proception. No perspective within the gross domain is more or less "close" to the proceiver. Nor is the proceiver ever more or less close to "nature," for proception itself is one natural process among an indefinite number of natural processes. The distinction which breeds this entire problem as its corollary difficulty—the distinction between the immediate and the mediate in experience—is a treacherous and deceptive one. It suggests that the world unjudged or merely felt and the world judged or interpreted are of disparate ontological status. (There is, indeed, a sense in which there are two worlds that are not the "same": there is a distinction between the world-unproceived and the world-proceived; but this means simply that the world can be proceived or can remain unproceived.) The better distinction would be between the objective relation which issues in inarticulate feeling and the objective relation which issues in judgment. Such a distinction is consistent with the different and more general distinction between objects and procepts, for a procept is an object or other natural complex in effective relation (in the sense defined) to a proceiver.

When experience is regarded as environmental "transaction" (Dewey) it successfully avoids the notion of a field of consciousness, but it lends itself, at the other extreme, to an emphasis upon the primacy of manipulation. It stands in need of a distinction between "felt immediacy" and proceptive assimilation. From the present standpoint, experience in this sense is more adequately conceived as the proceptive process. Just as it is important not to confuse assimilation with mere sensation, so it is important to construe manipulation not reductively in biologistic terms but as characterizing even the most abstract of intellectual operations.

Experience would then be the directed, cumulative interplay of assimilation and manipulation. The "data" of experience would be the events and objects, the natural complexes which, in relation to each individual, determine an indefinite class of procepts. Each man's procepts would constitute the "content" of *his* experience; the order or structure of his experience would be the proceptive domain; and the process or movement of his experience would be the proceptive direction. We have already suggested that in terms of the concept of proception the term "experience" would not need to be used at all. But in any event, experience is to be defined in terms of proception, not proception in terms of experience. This applies not only to refined philosophic uses of the term but to such well-established uses as are indicated by the phrases "the experience of the race" and "the appeal to experience." The first phrase has many possible translations: in one of its senses it refers to a class of *situations available* to any individual's proception; in another it refers to an accumulated body of *judgments characteristic* of any individual's proception. The second phrase, as incorporated, for instance, in the statement "Science appeals to experience," is in one sense absurd. There is no one who does not "appeal" to experience in the sense defined above; for no one is there a world other than the world he proceives. What is ordinarily intended by the usage is the appeal to certain formalized or semiformalized techniques of manipulation. This is clear when the term "observation" is used instead of "experience." Sometimes, however, a distinction is intended between

"private" (or "internal") and "public" experience, and
the "appeal" is said to be to the latter.

The distinction between public and private experience is not a distinction, antecedently determinable,
between two intrinsically different types of procepts,
or between two separate and irreconcilable "realms."
Any natural complex may become a procept for one or
more individuals, and may be designated by a common
symbol. In so far as this complex is or has been described or otherwise identified in common, it is public;
in so far as it has not been described or otherwise identified in common, it is private. Thus a natural complex
becomes, for certain individuals, a procept designated
by a common name—"toothache." To the extent that
communication effects a common description, the "experience" is public; to the extent that it does not, the
experience is private. This distinction applies to any
natural complex whatever. The reason why a rainfall is
held to be an intrinsically public experience is that we
conventionally ignore the existence of those responses
to rainfall which do not issue in the conventional identifications or descriptions. Some experiences, even in so
far as they are private, are ordinarily deemed *universal*
because, like "toothache," they are subjects of common
symbolization. Other experiences are neither coopera-
tively described nor conventionally classified; such experiences would be as yet neither public nor universal.

We are not justified by any evidence in speaking of
some procepts as not being natural complexes. For this
would mean that there is a realm of procepts which
have no conceivable or describable basis or source of

occurrence and which nevertheless modify or sustain a proceptive direction. The "purely private" in this sense of the term has been an obscurantist notion not only in psychology and theology but in the methodology of human experience. At bottom it is an invocation of the miraculous, whether it takes the form of divine illumination, ineffable truth, an impenetrable subconscious, or causally unaccountable sense-data. A distinction between public and private does not affect the interpretation of experience as, in the most fundamental sense, an interplay of manipulation and assimilation. Reverie, anguish, or toothache, in so far as they are private, are forms of assimilation in part dependent upon prior or present forms of manipulation—the manipulation, for instance, of my own body, of symbols in my thinking, of physical objects, or of other persons and their affairs. Nature is always the subject matter; experience is nature proceived.

II
COMMUNICATION

PROCEPTION AND COMMUNICATION, though distinguishable, presuppose each other. Without communication proception would be little more than protoplasmic endurance. Communication, on the other hand, requires individual direction, unless we assume a society of angelic forms which communicate by eternal inspection of their common essence. The entrance of an individual into the world is the advent of a process of assimilation: nature and history begin to communicate their burden to him; he begins by accepting a world in which his procepts include no utterances by him, and in which the manipulative side of his being is random. Whatever communication may be, it is at least a process of transmission. Older writers could speak of one object as communicating motion to another. We incline now to think of communication in terms of mutuality, possibly because a eulogistic note has crept into the concept. In one sense, whatever becomes a procept for the individual is communicated to him by nature or by art. The ocean communicates its vastness; history and the history of one's time communicate in the sense that they transmit symbols for proceptive assimilation. To the historian the past not only communicates but communicates directly; it not only affects but dominates his proceptive direction. The historian, the scientist generally speaking, interrogates nature (to use Kant's* great met-

* See Appendix.

aphor) for what it *can* communicate. He cannot communicate to nature because there is no individual, no direction that he can address or affect. Yet it seems undesirable to say, in needless dread of animism, that in reality neither do history and the ocean communicate to him but that he communicates with himself. He does, indeed, communicate with himself, in addition. The compulsion which nature exercises upon us and which effects invention in us is not transmission with intent— it is not a Berkeleyan world of signs antecedently willed and determined by God for presentation to mind—but neither is it an unqualified or simple instance of causal impact. If proceivers are involved, the causal situation is of a distinctive category.

These instances of asymmetrical communication may be distinguished from mere causal impact—that is, communicated procepts may be distinguished from mere procepts—by the condition that they generate signs. (What is called "mass-communication" is nonsymmetrical: the impact that generates signs may or may not be reciprocal.) Anything, in this sense, communicates to an individual if, in consequence of its impact, he directly begins to communicate with himself about it. I say "begins to" because a communicative process can be of indefinite duration. And I say "directly" because if we included merely the eventual possibility of its becoming the element of a future sign-complex for the individual, we should be unable to distinguish mere impact from communicative impact. Any natural impact at all is a potential sign-situation or is usable for further communication. The distinction is a difficult one. And it is difficult because there is no way of determining precisely the limits or the extent of a sign-situation. When we consider that species of communication wherein an individual alone utilizes and interprets signs, or communicates with himself—I shall call this reflexive communication—we see at once that any attempt to determine an instance of sign-manipulation is relative to some cross section of the proceptive domain. What does not at once become transformed into a subject of reflexive communication may invade or compel the proceptive domain by accretion and slow influence, and may form a subject of which other subjects are elements or moments. The character of reflexive communication in the floating domain may or may not be representative of that in the gross domain. When I speak of "reflexive communication" I am not simply using a verbose equivalent for "reflection." For, first, the latter term suggests either an intellectual operation or a technique for problem-solving, and therefore lacks the generality at which the present theory aims; and, second, it fails to suggest (even though it may not deny) a continuity between a proceptive and a social process.

The creative artist may be said to communicate asymmetrically with the spectator by contributing new elements for proceptive assimilation and manipulation. Response to a work of art is critical or noncritical depending on the extent to which the work, as subject, dominates reflexive communication. The effect of a work of art is measurable by the degree to which, as a subject, it pervades communication, reflexive or social, and influences the subsequent character of communication and invention. Art cannot be said to communicate in the sense that it transmits a "theme" or "message." Not only is this accidental and occasional, or false as a generalization; but a product of art does not communicate univocally as a product of science does. Its proceptive effect is not definable by standard or specifiable procedures of manipulation. Yet it is inept to say that the sign-components of artistic products, unlike those of scientific products, are "ambiguous." Ambiguity is a property usually understood to apply in linguistic products, and even more particularly, in language of an assertive character. The import of an ambiguous sign depends upon its context. When a context is specified or identified, the sign becomes determinate, and the determinateness will be of one kind or another as the context is altered. In most works of art, however, any context is itself subject to the same degree of interpretative latitude as its ingredients. Asymmetrical communication, then, is best understood through its influence on subsequent communication, which is necessarily reflexive and possibly social. Artistic communication in particular is determinable by the extent to which the proceptive response itself becomes an art.

None of the greater human products communicates in the sense that it imparts a fixed message. What it communicates depends on human receptivity and cultural conditions. Its communication is a continuous process, not an instantaneous impact. The function of criticism in science, philosophy, or art is to serve as both medium and catalyst for this process. For criticism is articulation; articulation extends meaning. Acceptance or rejection of a product signifies something about the status or character of what is communicated, but nothing about its communicative power. Criticism delivers the products of communication; it does not adjudicate their destiny. Some products are exposed at birth, others nurtured. But some exposed products thrive and continue to communicate, while others, though nurtured, fail to sustain their communicative force.

Symmetrical communication is both a requirement of animal survival and an avenue of abstract knowledge. It is both the condition of awareness and the fruit of awareness. It presupposes community, and community presupposes sharing. Now in order that community should obtain, it is necessary that some natural complex be a dominant procept for more than one individual in the same respect. It can be said, of the proceptive domain, that it is always "dominated" by some procept, but dominance is always dominance in some respect. Strictly speaking, every procept is the dominant procept in some specific respect. By definition, every proceptive domain is unique. Uniqueness does not imply absence of similarity or community. It results from a combination of factors, not from an absolute atomicity, indivisibility or "simplicity." For individuality as an unanalyzable simple, for the existence of *any* allegedly unanalyzable simple, there has never been any evidence. A comparison is always possible between one combination of factors and another, between the role which an object or concept plays in one proceptive domain and in another. Proceptive directions may show a parallelism in a given respect. One man's striving, for instance, is not another's; but it may be the same kind of striving. If we can suppose that objects may resemble one another, or that symbolic systems may be isomorphic, we can suppose that proceptive directions may be parallel. Extreme nominalism is extreme absurdity.

Symmetrical communication presupposes not only community but a special mode of community, namely, joint manipulation and assimilation of signs correlated with the dominant procept. And yet community as such is not a sufficient condition for symmetrical communication. Each individual must also be a procept of the other. This does not, of course, mean that each must be a *per*cept of the other, or that each must be "directly aware" of the other. Such conditions, as we have seen, are only accidental or special conditions of proception. Equally limited and inessential as a property of communication is "role-taking."* Nor does communication necessarily imply any situational or temporal restriction. A given "instance" of communication, like love between two persons, may be predicable of the gross proceptive domain; it may have no situational locus of any lesser scope than that of the self in its total career. The mother and child who clasp each other more tightly when frightened communicate anxiety or solicitude. The intention to do so is indeed irrelevant; but more important is the fact that what is here (not unjustifiably) considered an "instance" or "act" of communication is part of a larger and more persistent order of communication. We are too likely to think of

* For further clarification of this term, please see Appendix.

signs as qualitative configurations that are directly manipulatable. But an embrace of lovers is no more of a sign than their whole commonly directed pattern of behavior. The purview of a sign may be restricted and precisely defined, especially where the sign is introduced by convention or resolution, as in a devised logical calculus. But it may also be indefinite and undelimited: the sign may be of a protracted character.

In every instance of social or symmetrical communication there is an implicit mutual demand. This demand is for proceptive articulation in the form of products, overt manifestations of proception. In clasping the child the mother is implicitly requesting the child to come closer, to act in this or that way, to adopt a policy of caution. The most highly refined form of communicatory demand is mutual interrogation. It is in the depth and power of interrogation that the depth and power of thought consists, whether it be individual or inter-proceptive. Misology, aversion to ideas, is aversion to self-interrogation. The Socratic method was both an exhortation to become free of this fear and an attempt to exhibit the value of the liberation. It sought to formalize interrogation, and by this means to remove the natural mist from symmetrical communication.

Some philosophers think that communication is inexplicable unless we assume a "transcendent mind" common to the communicants.[2] There must be a "metaphysical" community of minds, an "antecedent mutuality of mind" and not merely a "sociological community." Without such an assumption, it is held, communication can be described behaviorally and explained causally but cannot be made "intelligible"; we miss "real" communication and remain only with the outer aspect of it. Now a theory of this kind is irrefutable and unprovable. But it is important to indicate why it is gratuitous and unnecessary. Why is a sociological community less of a reality than a so-called metaphysical community? And why is a theory of a nontranscendent community less eligible to be characterized as the metaphysical explanation than that of a transcendent community? The answer, I think, reveals something illuminating about theories of this type. The view in question supposes, correctly and innocuously enough, that in communication there must be a mutuality. But, not satisfied with a mutuality discoverable in the process of communication, in the same way that the results of communication are, it seeks a mutuality that binds more literally. It supposes a transcendent whole of which the communicants are literally parts. The irony is that in postulating such a self it is proceeding on a habit of thinking which is nominalistic and sensationalistic in a far greater degree than that which it seeks to avoid. It looks for mutuality in a kind of geometrical sense, where the parts are "really" parts. In the positing of a "common" self it is influenced by the pictorial habit of speculation. The mutuality envisaged is the unity of actual connection, of binding in the sense of contiguity—not spatial, to be sure, but pseudospatial—*some* kind of contiguity which to the sensationalist approach is the sole guarantee of "real" continuity. Only a concrete self, simply and numerically identifiable as one, can explain "real unity."

The postulation of transcendent entities on the basis of a covert sensationalistic method is not rare in philosophy. It is a congenial device in the history of classical rationalism and religious anthropomorphism.

The communicatory process can be misrepresented not only by gratuitous hypostatizations but also by theories of a naturalistic stamp. No one any longer can doubt the explanatory utility of behavioristic categories. They make it possible to show the factors common to physical contact on the one hand and human communication on the other. But they fail to supply an adequate differentia for the latter. It is not bodies which communicate any more than it is minds; and it is even unsatisfactory to say that it is men who communicate, if we persist in an inadequate theory of individuality. Communication is always more than simply a "conversation of gestures." The communicator is the proceiver: when we say that individuals are the relata of communication we must mean individual histories, and, more to the point, individual histories cumulatively represented. In addition, we must imply the presence in the individual of communal traditions—communities cumulatively reflected. In every communicative situation the individual detaches himself in some degree from all communities, even from that in which he is directly involved by the communication itself. This follows from the sheer fact of his own uniqueness or distinctiveness. He even becomes removed, in a sense, from his own self, from the burden of his proceptive direction, for the same reason that the particular is more than an instance of the universal. In one sense the imminent proceptive domain can *never* be fully representative of the gross domain. From any given community the individual can deliberately abstract himself, and from his own proceptive direction the individual can fancy himself aloof. But just as at the one end of the scale there is an inevitable distinctiveness, so at the other end there is a necessary and inevitable conformity. The revolution can never be complete, whether from the community or from the proceptive direction. Social and reflexive continuity are conditions of individuality. Alteration of the proceptive domain presupposes identification with it, and some community the individual must retain, since community and history are ingredients of the self.

The mutuality or community presupposed by communication is of two kinds, antecedent and contingent. The antecedent mutuality of those who communicate is, as it were, their hereditary community—national language, customs, moral standards, prepared attitudes. Over this community it is hardly possible to speak of control; even revolt implies and utilizes it. Such antecedent community is once removed from a potential communication situation. The proximate condition is a mutuality of contingent possessions: common possessions which explain the specific character of an instance of communication, though not necessarily its occurrence. Similar convictions shaped by a political atmosphere, joint involvement in a catastrophe, or chance bodily contact may determine the conditions for proceptive parallelism (in some respect) and for the circumstance under which each agent becomes a procept of the other. Contingent possessions ordinarily emerge out of prior communication situations.

Any number of diverse objects can be grouped into a class, because among any number of objects it is always possible to find a common characteristic. A community is not simply a class but, specifically, a class of proceivers (necessary condition) for whom a given natural complex functions as a dominant procept (sufficient condition). Community issues in communication when the further conditions obtain, that at least two proceivers become procepts of one another, and that they jointly manipulate the same set of signs. Mere community may be an enemy of communication. What men hold in common may alienate them from one another. It may diminish the force which makes for mutual demand. Community in one respect may conflict with community in another. Which community is the stronger determines the potentiality of communication.

The individual in himself constitutes a community, the reflexive or proceptive community. Logically and genetically, the reflexive community presupposes a social community. The soul converses with itself, as the *Theaetetus* says; but it also articulates itself, wars with itself, consoles itself, and fools itself. It is a community not of just two roles but of at least two roles. It may be a mystery how the Christian God can be three and one, but not how the proceiver can be. Intra-proceptive multiplicity is found by Mead in the assumption of different roles of an "other," and by James in the self's differing relational strategies. This multiplicity

follows from the relative alterability of the floating domain and the relative constancy of the gross domain.
Reflexive communication actualizes the reflexive community. This community is the final court of appeal in
all issues concerning decision and belief. No matter
how influential the forces of a social community may
be, it is for the individual to succumb and conform or
to protest and rebel.

> Adventure most unto itself
> The Soul condemned to be;
> Attended by a Single Hound—
> Its own Identity. *

The reflexive community holds the seeds of judgment,
no matter how implicit, blind, or coerced. The individual accumulates and transmits to himself a fund in
memory and potentiality, as the social community transmits to him its heritage in history. Both the individual
and society can interpret and misinterpret their past;
both must adopt guiding principles. Both are characterized by a guiding moral tone, that of the individual reflecting the proceptive direction, that of society reflecting the accumulated structure of its institutions.[3]

Individuality as an ingredient of nature becomes
most impressive when it is realized that what makes the
being of any community is not so much the homo-
geneity of individuals as the potency for many individuals of a given natural complex. When a community is
intense and rigid, when its bonds are grounded in dedication, this is not because individuality is minimized
but because the power of something common to indi-

* See Appendix.

viduals can be appropriated by each individual to conquer or alter his proceptive inertia, the course of his present self.

The individual belongs to many communities visible and invisible—to communities for which the defining circumstance is publicly articulated and to those for which it is not. Since some communities are stronger than others, there must be for each individual a hierarchy of allegiances. The bond of a community may be a bond of one individual to others, or a bond that ties an individual to the life and welfare of the collectivity of individuals—to the "community itself." A statesman's bond may be with the nation and not with other statesmen; a father's, with other fathers rather than with the institution of fatherhood. One is a collective, the other a distributive bond. A scientist may be tied both to science and to other scientists. The strength of a bond lies ultimately in the nature of the proceptive domain and the proceptive direction. The power of that which is common is relative to the individuals for whom it is common. That the character of proception is always in part and often in its entirety determined by a social community is unquestionable; yet the bond of the community is itself determined by the force and permanence of this influence. The creature may destroy the creator, and the individual may destroy the community. The potentially precarious relation of the individual to a particular community results from the fact that he is a crossroads of many communities. The wealth of the reflexive community depends on the wealth of the intersecting communities. Individuality is not to be identified with monotonous singleness or co-herency. On the contrary, it is only when the many communities become standard and homogeneous, or when they are rendered so by authority, that the indi-vidual solidifies his unity and loses his individuality.

Membership in a community does not necessarily involve either conscious alliance or, as Royce supposed, loyalty. I would, at least for the present purpose, distin-guish between allegiance and loyalty, the former to be understood in a metaphysical, the latter in a moral, sense. To be in or of a community may certainly entail attachment and striving; it must entail a proceptive parallelism of some extent. Whether or not community obtains is independent of the sense of loyalty. Procep-tive directions are irresistibly objective. They alone de-termine the existence of an invisible community. And if loyalty, group-awareness, and sense of tradition are inessential, it follows that communities do not neces-sarily have histories, as Royce thought they have, de-spite the fact that their members must. There are in-deed "communities of memory" and "communities of expectation," but there are also communities of neither kind. For Royce the idea of community, while not an exclusively moral idea, is inherently honorific; and the idea of an invisible community is necessarily "superhuman." This is understandable enough in the framework of an optimistic metaphysics which, strug-gling to invest Christianity with utmost persuasiveness, and to lay more than verbal emphasis on love, makes of love an indispensable ingredient in the concept of community. Community gives metaphysical support to love, receiving in return religious support from faith and hope.

But the invisible community is more silent and more earthly than Royce supposed. It is invisible not simply because of the limitations in awareness by the faithful, but because of the crude natural edges of individuality and the stubborn pervasiveness of nature. There are many invisible communities, not one; and there are trivial as well as exalted ones. Not all communities are sublime: the tendency to think so stems from the view that all are objects of loyalty, "causes." What makes the invisible community genuine is the real potentiality for unanimous action or feeling. There have been invisible communities of aggrieved peasants and criminal adventurers, but also of pigeon fanciers and sad men. There is a sense in which an invisible community never ceases to be invisible. The stimulus to community may come from an existing social organization perpetuating and enlarging itself, or mending its body, like the church; or it may come from proceptive processes in so far as they have arrived at a certain stage. Theological tradition to the contrary notwithstanding, it is in the latter case only that we can speak of an invisible community. In the former, the death of the social structure can destroy the community; in the latter, community is not contingent upon a social structure. It has its roots in reflexive communities and is not just mirrored in them. When the invisible community becomes visible as well, the outward recognition of community, the articulation of the existing bond, opens up an enormous range of possibility. The consequence may be social or intellectual action serving as outward symbol, or it may be external distraction to the real basis of community. In any event, the strength of a community does not lie in the sense of union that happens to prevail—sense of any kind may be fickle, fragile—nor in the external symbols of unanimity; it lies rather in the strength of each of the parallel proceptive directions. This does not mean that the reflexive community is separable from the multiplicity of visible communities, the individual from his social institutions. Great self-consciousness in the proceptive direction is rare, and it need not be denied that for the most part men are semimechanical products of social or mechanical forces. But this is simply to say that many communities intersect in the reflexive community, and that their impact and profusion is largely independent of individual control. It does not erase the distinction between the visible and the invisible community, nor the fact that the latter is the more tenacious and permanent in the lives of men. The movement of history is determined as much by invisible as by visible communities. The former reflect the more enduring phases of human nature as well as its inevitable subdivision into human types.

In one sense every community is less than visible. Allegiances are procepts, and no procept is fully visible in its ultimate destiny. A community can never be here-and-now. Its members are never perfectly and definitively "present" in respect of their community. They can never constitute a chorus which affirms the dominance of a procept with simultaneous accent or simultaneous awareness. The bonds of a community, like the limits of a proceptive domain, undulate. The community and its members are "in" one another, but with varying efficacy. We stand in more communities than we know, and often with a firmness that is greater or less than we suspect. Allegiance may be imprecise, and may consist in animal conservatism or tenacity; or it may consist, at the other end of the scale, in fierce martyrdom. It is a remarkable property of proception that allegiance does not depend on the proximity or tangibility of the object. This can be seen especially in certain forms of religious community. The source of faith has often been an imperative couched in logical obscurity and historical mystery. Analysis, logical suasion, can destroy a loyalty; but it can also reinforce one by challenging its endurance, so that the object of faith becomes faith itself.

The property of communication can distinguish proception from mere biological perseverance only in so far as something emanates from it. In the life of man all things are either subjects or products of communication. Nature, as it were, provides all subjects. The domain of the actual subjects is the measure of man's impact on nature and of the ways in which he has assimilated nature. The products of communication constitute the realm of human creation, man's addition to nature; or, otherwise expressed, the transformation of natural properties and the actualization of natural potentialities.

Every living moment represents an implicit discovery.

What is commonly singled out as the object or occasion of discovery is the novel, but it is plain that the novel is always embedded in a familiar framework, and that all things familiar are novel in some perspective. The novel is the development in the old of an unexpected significance, or the appearance in the old of a trait that cannot immediately be reconciled with its official essence. Discovery, then, is inevitable. Significant discovery requires utterance for its delivery. Utterance is no less primordial and no less inevitable, though in common usage it bears much less of a eulogistic flavor. It is a relation between proception and production: procepts, by one or another mode of combination, give rise to products. The leap by which natural complexes assume a role in the human direction or by which they are utilized and represented, and the leap by which utterance is born, are the most rudimentary steps in technology or the economy of manipulation. If utterance is the natural manifestation of discovery, articulation is the fulfillment of utterance. On the usual view, what we articulate are words and what we do when we articulate is to clarify or illuminate verbal meanings. There is no reason why all signs whatever may not be articulated. But more fundamentally, there is no reason why all products whatever may not be said to be susceptible of articulation. Articulation is the manipulation (and the implied proceptive deliverance) of products as ends in themselves, that is, as subjects of communication for the sake only of further communication.

Traditionally a distinction is made between products, acts, and assertions. In Aristotle, this takes the form of the threefold distinction between productive, practical, and theoretical science. But regardless of the undoubted admissibility and utility of such a distinction, we can with superior generality regard whatever emanates from any proceptive domain as a product. Acts and assertions are products no less than sensuous configurations of material are. The same applies to the constituents of acts, such as movements and gestures, and to the constituents of assertions, such as words and other types of signs. The tendency to distinguish between actions and products stems from the natural and altogether defensible distinction between doing and making. But in terms of the category of proception specific instances of doing and making are seen to emerge from the same cumulative process. What is done and what is made are equally symptomatic of the world that is proceived.

Merely to discern the status as products of all of the ultimate human materials for communication, and to recognize products as proceptive transformations, is not yet sufficiently clarifying. The product, representing nature re-created by human nature, has a voice. Nature refashioned is nature interpreted. Every product is a judgment. A judgment is a pronouncement: every product is a commentary on the proceiver's world as well as a faint image of the proceptive direction. It is a version, a rendition of nature, born of manipulation. Human utterance cannot be understood solely in terms of assertion, for every product that emanates from proception and communication is as much a precept-transformation as any other. Any product, moreover, can function to communicate. We cannot arbitrarily or antecedently limit what may and what may not function as a sign. A medieval cathedral is not a malleable instrument of direct or intended communication, but it would be folly to deny that its historical burden carries meaning and that this meaning is continually operative. An exclamation may communicate more than a declaration, and a gesture may influence understanding more than a verbal explanation.

To speak of products and judgments, then, is one and the same thing; but the former term suggests the source and the natural history of man's concretizations,* while the latter suggests their ultimate function, status, and direction. In looking upon every product as judicative, it becomes necessary to explain the sense in which non-assertive products share the same basic properties as assertive. Human judgment appears to be of three kinds, which we may call assertive, active, and exhibitive. Assertive judgments include all products of which a certain type of question is ordinarily asked: Is it true or false? Exhibitive judgments include all products which result from the shaping or arranging of materials (and these materials include humanly shaped signs). Active judgments comprise all instances of conduct to which the terms "act" or "action" are ordinarily applied. The difficulty of drawing sharp lines among these classes is obvious. The distinctions are not primarily structural but functional. Whether certain gestures are acts, or whether they are assertions in an unconventional medium, depends partly upon the context of utterance and partly upon emphasis and communicative intent. The extent to which a literary work is assertive

* For further clarification of this term, please see Appendix.

and the extent to which it is exhibitive depends upon similar factors. A "proposition" is an assertion; but its proceptive location or its place in a larger propositional scheme may give it an active or an exhibitive role. A "propositional function" is potentially assertive, but primarily exhibitive of a propositional structure. An exclamation may be an exhibitive judgment to the extent that it crystallizes an emotion in verbal form; an active judgment to the extent that it is the behavioral response to a situation; and an assertive judgment to the extent that it describes a situation elliptically or covertly.

Some philosophers would doubtless want to distinguish emphatically between assertions and the other two types of products. They would want to regard only the former as judgments on the ground that these alone are instruments of communication, while the other products function as means of stimulation. In an assertion, presumably, there is a "content" transmitted, and a content delimits the sphere of interpretation; whereas in the case of the other products interpretation is not called for by the product as such but is only an accidental concomitant or behavioral response. But to accept this distinction is to be committed, in the first place, to a dubious notion of "content." Any product has content in so far as it *is* interpreted. The real difference is that from a linguistic assertion the content is traditionally something expected, and there is much greater unanimity on the correlation of a given content with the given linguistic utterance. That language as we ordinarily understand the term has numerous special advantages for communication, such as susceptibility to abstraction and to easy manipulation in the economy of thought, no one would wish to deny. But assertion and linguistic assertion are hardly synonymous. Those who think of human judgment solely in assertive terms cannot appeal solely to the properties of language to warrant the restriction. For many types of behavior can be and are deliberately intended to function assertively.

Whoever thinks of communication as effected by assertion alone greatly oversimplifies the notion of assertion and communication alike. The individual who understands, whose proceptive domain is influenced by a human product, is not a target on whom a mark is made, nor a receptacle in which an object is deposited. What the traditional epistemology of consciousness and conscious contents obscures is the fact that symmetrical communication is a relation between proceivers. Assertive judgments are too often regarded as discrete vehicles of meaning, transmitted by one agent and accepted by another. It might appear that ordinary verbal exchange is largely of this character. But even an elementary mode of communication is made possible by the proceptive disposition of the assimilator. And where two highly articulate persons fail to achieve rapport, proceptive divergence is responsible. Communication can be limited or can be actually impossible even after endless dialectic, not because of the absence of any mysterious affinity that is the alleged *sine qua non,* but because certain conditions required by the situation remain unfulfilled. The simplest type of assertion presupposes the power of symbolic identification, however habitual this may be. Whether judgment be assertive or non-assertive, then, identification, grouping, and inference are elemental requisites of the recipient; and these are proceptive phenomena.

A judgment is a selection, discrimination, or combination of (natural) characters, rendered proceptively available. No product can be more of a selection and discrimination of characters than any other, and this is why no one type of judgment is more fundamental than any other. The trouble with older conceptions of "judgment" is that they incline to identify it as intellectual utterance—"utterance" and "intellectual utterance" are tacitly equated—or as an entity of a peculiarly "mental" status, as the product of that dimension of the individual in which utterance is supposed to be possible. But utterance in the human individual is proceptive, and hence multifarious; and utterance which is inter-individual results not from a community of minds but from a community.

The most commonplace of active judgments, such as walking from one place to another, represents selection and discrimination by the walker, though not necessarily, of course, on the level of deliberate awareness or self-conscious representation. We have already had sufficient evidence that conscious awareness is not a basic category so far as the natural foundations of utterance are concerned. Neither active judgments nor the other modes of judgment derive their judicative character from a concomitant fact of awareness but rather from the fact that they are periodical expressions of the ongoing interplay of assimilation and manipulation. What is fundamental is not that each product is reflexively represented (by the producer) but that each is representable or interpretable. The former circumstance is occasional, the latter essential to judgment. Every product is a judgment precisely because it offers itself, as product, for interpretation and appraisal. Thus a work of art, whether a mechanically produced chest of drawers or a poem, invites interpretation or assimilation by exploiting natural complexes and through them contriving a determinate or unitary order. It is usually exhibitive rather than assertive or active: that is, it does not call primarily or at all for interpretation in terms of truth or falsity, nor for interpretation in terms of expediency or rightness in the pattern of conduct. What it calls for minimally (certainly not exclusively) is approbation and assimilation in respect of the combination of characters as such. In so far as a work of art is interpretable in terms, say, of its moral implications, it is an active judgment; in so far as it is interpretable in terms of its influence on the type of cognitive enterprise known as factual inquiry, it is assertive. No product is intrinsically active, assertive, or exhibitive: its judicative function is determined by its proceptive or communicative context.

The judgments of man are not only commentaries on the world; they are the only devices by which process is arrested and appropriated. They are crystallized manipulations. But they function also to render nature assimilable. The world of judgments is not just nature pictured—the metaphysical difficulty inhering in such an account is notorious—but nature, as it were, in process of self-illumination. Judgment, however, is more than the vehicle by which life distinctively human is made possible. It is the means by which nature allows the individual to transcend himself. Through each product the individual is literally multiplied. In reflexive communication he multiplies the dimensions of his individuality, in social communication he makes possible new life and growth.* But it is in the very occurrence of the product that self-transcendence is potential. True, the great majority of products originate and die inconsequentially in this or that proceptive domain. Yet each product, in so far as it is a judgment, is so to speak more than a mere product. The product is an event in time; the judgment is eternal in that the circumstances of its origin do not comprehend its entire being. There can be no assurance that any judgment is mortal or infertile. It always represents in its utterance more than it reflects in its occurrence. And yet the individual or the community is not just a natural seedbed for an instrument that becomes miraculously self-sufficient. It will become clear from our analysis of perspective that the judgment is not separable from any of an indefinite number of networks, so that its potential universality may be said to be one and the same with that which resides naturally within the individual.

Some procepts become subjects of reflexive communication, others do not. A burn unnoticed might fall in the latter class, the moon as an object of study in the former. In other words, some procepts become represented as elements of sign-complexes, which may be called projects. All products are ultimately the outcome of the proceptive direction, but not all are necessarily the outcome of reflexive communication, that is, of pro-

* For further clarification of these terms, please see Appendix.

jects. The latter products are products of *query:* * they comprise the judgments of the arts and of the sciences, and in general all judgments that emanate from constructive probing. A project, or distinguishable instance of query, already involves judgments; it is itself a product—one not yet universally available. Not every project actually culminates in a socially available product; and in fact it is doubtful that any product of query can be considered the outcome of a "single" project. And if this is so, the line between products of query and other products is not a sharp one, despite the usefulness of the distinction.

Signs are essential to communication, but it is a mistake to think that the materials of communication are exclusively signs, if by a "sign" we understand that which serves to represent or interpret a natural complex and which is itself interpretable. Only abstract thinking involves signs exclusively; communication, the guiding mechanism of proception, is a much more pervasive and fundamental process. Physical objects may be direct materials of communication, no less than they may be direct materials for perception or observation. When I contemplate a house under construction and reflect upon it, weighing its merits, comparing it with other houses, and bringing standards to bear upon it, the house is as much a part of the project in my query as the signs conjoined with it. This is precisely what is to be understood when we say that the house is a procept for me. Projects and other products are procept-transformations in the sense that they are alterations of my relation to the object. In any case, objects-in-

* For further clarification of this term, please see Appendix.

relation-to-me are the materials of both reflexive and social communication, along with the instruments by which they are representable (the signs). Both the objects and the signs which represent them are pro-cepts: both are natural complexes bearing upon the proceptive direction.

The house itself may have a representative function: it may function as a sign. But it may not. When I dis-cuss the house-in-process with another spectator, it is as much a means of communication as the other ingre-dients of the analysis. The supposition that only signs are involved in communication arises partly from the tendency to think of signs as portable vehicles, but more subtly, from the view that the subjects of com-munication are mutually transferred or literally shared (and in the case of reflexive communication, posited at will and dismissed at will from consideration). This supposition is rendered plausible by the correlative supposition that communication is between minds and that therefore it is not the house but only a sense-image, idea, or concept that can be "in the mind" at all. Thus there is apparent justification for the view that com-munication is "about" the house, that the house "itself" is not "communicated." But in the very same sense, neither are the symbols employed by the analysis "com-municated" in the sense of being actually given by one to another. The communicators *refer* to the symbols no less than to the house, and they *utilize* the house no less than the symbols. Thus the house is part of the project of reflexive communication in two proceivers and of the social communication in which they are engaged, and the judgments made about the house constitute the products of the communication.

Now it is the house witnessed, not the house financed or the house originally conceived that is here part of the project. Some philosophers cannot abide the view that it is the *house* we witness. They feel that it is only a sense-datum or essence or appearance or image that enters as the subject of communication or as the direct object of attention. When I recede from the house, the "house" grows smaller—but not the "real" house, only an image of the house; the smallness belongs to the sensum, the idea. This way of speaking is gratuitous, to say the least: we can certainly discard the assumption of a distinction between appearance and reality in favor of an assumption that the house really changes its properties in different perspectives. The house unquestionably grows smaller in the perspective of vision. That is to say, under the conditions of backward movement on my part, it occupies less and less of a place in the visual field. At the same time it remains the same size in the perspective of physical measurement with respect to mass or shape. Not only are both judgments consistent; the qualifications introduced actually make it possible to predict one from the knowledge of the other. The philosophers who find it necessary to distinguish between posited objects and perceptual apearances have been likely to find the object twice removed in their philosophic reckoning: as the idea is necessarily proxy for the thing, so the sign must necessarily designate the idea. Presumably we communicate about our own products directly and about the world only remotely.

Not that anyone who suffers and aspires in this life can take such an implication and such a position seriously in his waking moments. A world which creates and destroys men, and amidst the indifferent circumstances of which communication is born and is permitted, can hardly be so distant as their epistemologies would believe.

III
COMPULSION

THE SPECIFIC PRODUCTS OF COMMUNICATION go into the making of a grand product, the fabric of societized man. They are not sufficient conditions: procepts as well as products are required, and the products of man comprise only one set of procepts among the numerous sets that nature generates. Communication is a circular process. It feeds on procepts (products of nature and of man) and breeds products which enhance the number and variety of its future procepts. Some of these products, like the commonplace judgments of daily intercourse, simply contribute to the perpetuation of a community; others, like the creations of art or law, provide human life, for better and for worse, with its qualitative potentialities.

There are two principal modes in which the proceiver judges relative to the world and to the products of communication: one is by compulsion, the other by convention. Through compulsion he responds to an uncontrollable situation; through convention he selects from alternatives. Through the one he conforms to what the nature of things (including the products of man) imposes; through the other he hovers among what the nature of things offers. These categories remain to be clarified, but one possible initial difficulty may be eliminated immediately. The concept of compulsion is not to be identified with that of "determination," nor the concept of convention with that of "freedom"; and in general, any similar contrast between, say, necessity and freedom or external determination and self-determination is irrelevant to the present distinction. Both types of categories are indeed metaphysical categories, because of their level of generality. But compulsion and convention are to be understood in terms of proception, not in terms of a problem of causality. In any event, freedom is to determination as species to genus, while compulsion and convention are parallel categories equally fundamental for the analysis of proception and communication. It is possible, and from one point of view necessary, to speak of "causal compulsion"; but, in the present usage, a distinction would still have to be made between causal and other types of compulsion. Causal compulsion may or may not be present in any other type; it is certainly not the type to which any other can be reduced. Consider, for example, the compulsion involved in envy. The situation of envy contains causal elements, and a chain of causes renders the emotion possible. But the compulsion involved is more than merely causal: it is, for one thing, biological in character (there are causal compulsions which are not of a biological character); or, it may be regarded as having biological, social, moral, and psychological dimensions; and these require independent analysis over and above their causal factors.

Compulsion is present in so many ways, in so many specific contexts that it is futile to attempt any classification. When sugar is tasted, sweetness is a compulsive effect; when we slip in the middle of the road, scrambling to our feet is a compulsive means or condition of safety; when we accept certain assumptions, we are compelled to accept certain conclusions; certain alternatives irresistibly exclude or demand other alternatives; certain disorders of a neurotic character compel specific forms of behavior. Compulsions are very different in character, and in one sense perhaps different in degree. But in all cases the judgment involved is the sole product possible for a given proceptive domain. A conventional judgment is the relatively indifferent product among a possible group of alternatives. These are brief formulations, and "possible" does not mean "logically possible" or theoretically conceivable. A better formulation would be: In so far as a judgment can be regarded as the sole product congruous with a given proceptive domain, it is compulsive; otherwise, it is conventional.

Recognition of compulsion on this broader level helps to explain individual behavioral patterns and limitations, and it helps also to explain the occurrence and nature of social patterns and social conflict. We shall employ it here as a category in the metaphysics of communication and therefore as a means of clarifying the nature of human utterance.

Underlying all of the specific modes of compulsion that affect the individual is a blanket or gross compulsion. Notwithstanding the egoism of a technological age, the individual is allotted feeble powers by the nature of things, and moves in an environment largely uncontrollable. Truistically speaking, gross compulsion is equivalent to the finitude of the self, implying the restrictions that appertain *ipso facto* to a proceiver. But it has a vital and concrete character. No fact can be so alive to the individual as his own ultimate helplessness with respect to space, time, and matter, and his own immediate helplessness with respect to the traits of things and of persons. Gross compulsion is the irreversibility and sweep of the proceptive process. Ever-present and continually efficacious in the inertia of the proceptive direction, it exhibits itself as it were antecedently in the form of the channels prescribed by hereditary equipment and animal drives. It is not something that attacks the individual as a separate or distinct force; it is as essential to his being as the life of which it is an ingredient. Nor should it be confused with "impulse." One contemporary philosopher tells us that "All human activity springs from two sources: impulse and desire."[4] This is not so much a false statement as an oversimplification. Impulses men undoubtedly have, and perhaps even definitely directed impulses. But activity which would ordinarily be ascribed to a positive impulse is often better interpreted as a response than as a drive, as a struggle to stand up rather than as a readiness to run. For the most part, "activity" is best regarded as drawn from the individual rather than as contributed by him. The superiority of compulsion to impulse as a proceptive category appears most clearly in ethical analysis. Impulse as a "spring" of conduct implies too sharp a line between achievement and frustration. A given impulse is presumably either satisfied or curbed, either checked or not checked by desire and will. But achievement and frustration are not qualities of discrete drives; they are complex relational predicates. Moral development and unification (character) is not something that opposing impulses yield when they are neutralized or stabilized. It is not a residue but a proceptive dimension.

The "content" of proception is no less compulsive than the process—the domain no less than the direction. In one sense, all procepts are compulsive. This does not mean that recalcitrancy is the dominant quality of human experience. Recalcitrancy is a property that belongs to objects in so far as they are manipulated. Our manipulations are alternately successful and unsuccessful, and the object is recalcitrant in the degree to which they are unsuccessful. Gross compulsion is perhaps best understood by reference to the acceptive or assimilative side of our being. When we manipulate, we manipulate something whose properties we have accepted. Complete manipulation is none at all. This is the general categorial formulation of which the relation between law and liberty, determination and choice is a special application: we are said to be free relative to conditions of predictable pattern, and to make choices relative to limited alternatives. The idea of destiny is significant when defined in terms of gross compulsion. "What is to be" for the individual is neither foreordained nor preestablished. It is the force of the proceptive direction. Gross compulsion is not logical necessity but the efficacy of accumulated life. All procepts are compulsive in this sense, that, while objects are irrelevant and indifferent, procepts play a role and

as occurrents are final and irretrievable. They could even be defined as the natural complexes which compel living in the respect of reinforcing or altering its basic direction.

Gross compulsion is often the direct subject of awareness. This awareness takes the form of realizing the bounds and the essential fixity of the self. We often conclude, with respect to a given aspect of ourselves or with respect to our "nature," that we are "just like that" or "born that way" for better or worse. There is deep significance in this simple reflection. To a certain extent we transcend ourselves and even alter ourselves through self-appraisal, but we re-create neither ourselves nor the conditions of proception. Gross compulsion does not admit of degrees. What does admit of degrees is the quality of our felt responsiveness.

The importance of compulsion methodologically speaking is its role in the shaping of human products. Ontologically, the process of production is continuous; methodologically, it is a series of leaps or judgments. Each judgment is the expression of compulsion or convention. It is an embodiment or terminus of the proceptive direction, or, specifically, of the train of communication. Communication stops here and there, desists from or pursues such-and-such a path, ratifies, accepts and rejects. Judgments are decisions, for the most part of a rudimentary and implicit character. Communication may be more or less complex, it may involve a greater or lesser number of steps. But whatever its composition, it cannot culminate in a product unless it culminates in ratifications, decisions, assents—

that is to say, unless it evolves a means of making itself relatively complete. All judgments are relative completions. They are in one sense versions of the self in its relation to the world—representations of a proceiver—and every version is a relative termination, or expression of a perspective.

Compulsion may involve active, exhibitive, or assertive judgment. It may directly relate to the specific *circumstances* of action or to the *character* of action; it may directly relate to the specific circumstances of assertion or to its content. I say "directly relate to" as being more specific than and as implying something other than "affect." In the present sense of these terms, a law against monopolies would affect me but not directly relate to me. A compulsion may, of course, not only affect but directly relate to one and the same product. Purely physiological compulsion, for instance respiratory functioning, might affect the character of an action and an assertion but would not directly relate to them; it might directly relate to a circumstance rather than to a meaning. The compulsion exercised by a verbal threat might directly relate to the character of an action and an assertion, and not to specific circumstances of action and assertion; these it might only affect.

That which compels the character or content of a product may be said to compel methodologically; that which compels circumstantially or factually may be said to compel non-methodologically. Though the distinction is important, it is not always possible to draw the line sharply. The compulsion exercised by the bio-

logical situation of hunger would not, except accidentally, have a methodological significance. But it is more difficult to say this of the compulsion exercised, say, by the mores. Compulsion of any kind makes its final impact on the character of communication. But certain modes—the methodological—act by *means* of reflexive communication, while the others do not. Hunger ultimately affects communication but does not make itself felt in and through (or directly by means of) communication. The mores do in part. The compulsiveness of an argument that reveals us to be holding contradictory opinions exercises its force through reflexive communication. The compulsion of sense-experience is of a mixed kind, depending on what we emphasize. So far as it consists in mere response to a sensory quality through a sense organ, it is non-methodological. The effect is to arouse a brute feeling or, in perceptive awareness, a sense-judgment (for instance the explicit judgment "That's red" or the implicit judgment "Red!"). But if "sense-experience" be construed more broadly to include the effect of the sense-judgment itself, then in this judgment its methodological compulsion lies. Not brute feeling alone but the judicative articulation of feeling affects the nature of communication. The initially aroused sense-judgment may be considered either as a mere physiological effect or as a product with potentialities for communication, that is, retrospectively or prospectively. As a mere effect it does not, ontologically, differ from the stars seen after a blow on the head. What makes "sensation" stand out from other modes of compulsion is its close relation to the actual

process of exhibitive, active, or assertive judging.

Contrivance and inquiry, art and science, ultimately depend on the kind of assimilation by which a natural complex defines itself in reflexive communication. Without funded experience, accumulated knowledge, and the fortunate accidents of the present environment, no products would ever emerge and no projects would ever be inaugurated. Inventive communication arises only when a complex translates itself into reflexive compulsion. "Inward," reflexive compulsion of the kind that gives rise to products of query is the compulsion of imagination. Reflexive compulsion is the first labor pain of the process in which man contributes to nature out of what he has received from it. Inspiration and insight, though species of compulsion, are correctly regarded as species of spontaneity. They are compelled as distillates of a proceptive domain easy to recognize and difficult to characterize. The spontaneity lies in the novelty of the incipient project, rather than in the supposed randomness of its origin. If insight and inspiration do not always bear fruit, it is because compulsion does not imply consummation. Insight, however fragmentary, is itself a birth. It looks for articulation but does not ensure it.

Discovery, which is omnipresent and promiscuous, is the natural kin of all products and not just of products of query. But reflexive compulsion is a necessary condition of products of query and their incipient articulation. Why do we seek to articulate? Why do we seek to increase the fertility of our utterances? For the products of articulation yield new compulsion. If works of

art relieve us, they also constrain us; they impose a discipline of encounter and discernment. Theory, likewise, compels the direction of belief, defines its limits, and curbs the boundless lust of speculation. As the chain of judgment grows, the royal road turns into a jagged one. And yet it is compulsion that liberates. The assimilation of an exhibitive judgment is more intricate than the assimilation of an undifferentiated sensuous complex, but it is far more fundamental for the proceptive direction. Increase in the kinds and levels of assertive cognition* makes error more and more of a threat; but if we must encompass less, we may assert more. The products of articulation make rigorous claims upon the allegiances of man, but his freedom cannot be otherwise defined. Human invention is a process of seeking, and not merely of breeding, compulsion. For by the laws and forms of perception we define significant perception, and by the laws and patterns of belief we define true belief. Every determination is an exclusion, every definition a delimitation, every discovery a demarcation.

The end-results of communication, the framework within which we articulate, compel us in various directions. But query itself, the evolution of project into product, exhibits a distinctive compulsion, of a protracted kind. Works of art in process are guided by a theme or idea. The envisioned end imposes conditions on its own achievement. The end can be provisional, and the means actually employed can help to determine the actual being of the end. But plans impose curbs, and each modification in the plan imposes its own curbs.

* For further clarification of this term, please see Appendix.

Query is by definition a process of planning; but there is good reason for the definition. Planless creation is purposeless creation, and from purposeless creation the idea of reflexive communication would have to be excluded. Artistic query takes the forms of both overt and reflexive experimentation. In art, as in science, experiment test a proposal. Query is inventive manipulation.

The birth and execution of a product of query, the very germ and plan of it, ultimately come, as do all other products, from gross compulsion, from the uniqueness of a proceptive domain. Ordinarily the problem is posed, whether the products of science as well as of art can be said to reflect the individual as their ultimate source. In so far as the individual himself is, ontologically speaking, a product, he is not the ultimate source of the products either of art or science. But since the community and the proceiver presuppose each other, any product whether of science or art requires a proceptive domain for its genesis and locus. In both cases the gross compulsion is the same—what I am thus far is the ultimate compelling factor in what I judge now. Nevertheless, does the proceptive basis of the judgment color its status or meaning to a greater extent in art than in science? There are traditions in both art and science. But from the standpoint of antecedent influences on the individual, we can speak mainly of scholastic and cultural attachments in art, whereas in science we may (and perhaps must) speak of a dominating heritage that requires an underlying commitment. Prospectively, too, the artistic product may deviate in a way that the scientific may not: a scholastic attachment may be abandoned without loss; the scientific heritage is far more continuous both in content and in method. The artist can be a more spontaneous revolutionary, not perhaps in the degree of his innovation but in the extent of his deviation. The scientist must justify his judgments in the scientific community. He (or time) must resolve the discrepancy between the community and himself by either making it move in his direction or modifying his direction through a conviction of unanimity with it.

The scientist, like the artist, thinks in terms of specific projects and problems. That is to say, the conditions of his aim limit the character of his thinking, even beyond the limitations imposed by accumulated knowledge and the investigable traits of nature. Once he has begun to achieve explanation, the course of his thinking imposes a further compulsion: as the artist is dominated by the physical properties of his medium, the scientist is dominated by the principles of logic and mathematics. He is committed to a course of reasoning—to a specific course until he alters the direction of his initial imaginings; but to a general mode of reasoning no matter what his specific course may be or may have been. Logical compulsion—the compulsion imposed by the laws of logic—is an elemental framework within which proception and communication occur. Consistency is a condition of survival in utterance, exhibitive and active as well as assertive. While questions of consistency are not substantively applied in the non-assertive modes of utterance, there can be nothing in any judgment that actually refutes the law of contradiction. Inconsistent signs may be physically juxtaposed and even systematically manipulated by conventional resolution, but they achieve the status of meaningful entities in the system only through consistency or order in the manipulation. The laws of logic exercise a conspicuous compulsion: we cannot reject them and still retain intelligibility. In particular they ground discourse, for discourse cannot, as Aristotle showed, reject them without assuming them. It is hard to conceive circumstances under which they would be invalidated, for they are conditions of conceivability.

When Descartes instituted his drama of doubt, he was seeking to discover compulsiveness in judgment. By showing that this property lies at the basis of whatever we deem worthy of the name of knowledge, he evinced an insight largely overlooked by his classical successors who busily devoted themselves to the perpetuation of his psychologism. They might better have sought to clarify his confusions about the nature of compulsion in judgment and the logical status of the different types of belief; his failure to enumerate, besides the explicit beliefs to which inquiry is committed, the presuppositions that inquiry brings with it; his failure to realize that, although inquiry involves compulsion, this does not warrant the view that knowledge means infallible discernment.

Despite his constant appeal to the model of mathematics Descartes's conception of compulsion as irresistible clearness remained individualistic. Presumably the perceptiveness of enlightened men was of a single kind, and clearness was universally recognizable. But the criterion of recognizing it remained undefined. Descartes understood and framed the scientific dream but lost hold of the scientific method. Science is a quest for compulsive judgment. But how do its judgments achieve their status, and what are the kinds of compulsion essential to the scientific enterprise? The reflexive compulsion of insight is of a very peculiar kind when properly characterized as "scientific." The insight is generated in an atmosphere compounded of cordiality and hostility. It is not prized for the novelty of its sheer existence or for its impact on human sensibility. Its value lies in its service as a sacrifice for the illumination of other alternatives or as a compulsive candidate for validation. Scientific hypotheses compel, as it were, by indirection. They focus attention on some configuration in nature which is in itself non-refutable and inescapable though mute. They supply the formula of intelligibility without which the configuration is for us no configuration but an indeterminate complex. The compulsiveness of a theory is not rendered illusory by its potential alterability. And its scope is defined by the problem which gives rise to it: it explains at least as much as it is asked to explain. It is superseded or amended when the scientific demand develops for a breadth of explanation to which it is unfitted. A problem introduces the need for a revised perspective within some area of the scientific domain. A theory is the formal definition of a perspective. Its stability or relative validity depends upon the manner in which allied perspectives change. A theory may prove to be a sub-perspective within a larger perspective or theory; or it may prove to be incompatible with other sub-perspectives. More cannot be asked of a theory than that it be supported by the evidence that is available. "Available evidence" is really a redundant expression: unavailable data cannot serve to judge. Evidence is as treacherous as it is relentless. But the realization that our perspectives have been different in the past and may change in the future does not affect the compulsiveness of present evidence.

What is evidential compulsion? The various methods by which it is achieved—such as legal inquiry or common probable argumentation—are versions, applications, or informal embodiments of the method of science. But why is scientific confirmation universal, and why does the community of scientists inevitably move toward unanimity in the acceptance or rejection of a scientific product? Why do scientists understand one another to the maximum extent possible in communication? The answer ordinarily given is that science is essentially an appeal to experience, a submission to fact. Peirce preferred to define "experience" as "the compulsion, the absolute constraint upon us to think otherwise than we have been thinking."[5] This tells us little unless the mode of compulsion be clarified; for, as it stands, this criterion could be satisfied by social authority or indeed by almost any type of influence. Elsewhere Peirce defines the power of scientific judgment by the condition that it "be determined by nothing human, but by some external permanency—by something upon which our thinking has no effect."[6]

But it is not enough to say that experimental verification is universally intelligible and compulsive in virtue of what is "real" or "objective" or "there" for inevitable acceptance. Art and philosophy are concerned with what is "there," and both certainly involve an "appeal to experience"; yet they do not bring the same kind of compulsion. It must be that in the process of prediction theory touches an elemental ingredient in the proceptive direction of every man: his power and means of adjustive manipulation. What we call "evidence" compels by defining the adjustive limits of human action. It compels because it is a necessary condition of adaptation, exploration, and control. Nothing is so requisite to sanity as the estimate of reasonable control. Thus only the madman, intrinsically indecisive, can be deaf to the eloquence of experimental decision. But though he be unimpressed by the requirements of fact, he lives and gropes in accordance with these requirements. We cannot "disagree" with scientific inquiry; it is a formalization of our own proceptive demand for guidance among the complexes of fact.

Theoretical speculation in science is a manipulation of ideas. This manipulation takes various forms: calculation, linguistic determination, comparison, abstraction. It is in part random, in part planned juxtaposition and combination. Symbolic manipulation which is non-adjustive in character and which moves in the direction of increasing abstraction constitutes speculation in pure mathematics. In natural science, symbolic or "ideal" manipulation is a means to experimental manipulation. Experiment is the formal process of adjusting a given relation between ideas and facts. It is deliberative manipulation which minimizes spontaneity and commits itself to a supreme moral obligation of disinterestedness. The reward of disinterestedness is control. Before the scientist "controls" nature he must control his ideas. Experiment is cognitive control achieved by the marriage of disinterestedness with manipulative ingenuity. On the result of cognitive control depends technological control—manipulation in applied science.

The process of systematic or pursued assimilation in science is seen most clearly in the realm of theory. The content of ideas makes an impact during the entire process of ideal manipulation, and the impact is altered when the manipulation reaches its relative terminus. Systematic assimilation is contemplative vision. We are inclined to think of contemplation, in spite of Aristotle's view that it is a species of action, as a dumb seeing, and as a seeing of what is final or uncontrollable. But it is possible to have roving vision; and although no object of vision is final or uncontrollable in an absolute sense, there is another sense in which every phase or moment of vision has assimilative finality. In experiment the basic process of assimilation is no less fundamental, despite the change in the mode of manipulation. Experiment entails a special kind of contemplative quest in the process of devising, and not merely of using, new techniques for the testing of predictions. This quest requires ideal manipulation and ideal assimilation on a given level and with respect to a given problem. Nothing in science is more common than the occurrence of problems in the solution of problems. And in general, nothing is more common than the virtually indistinguishable collaboration of doing and accepting, of giving and seeing, not only in deliberative inquiry but in all of life and communication.

Science is a means of progressively stabilizing expectation and of discovering orders in nature and history. It dispels puzzlement, but like philosophy and art, it increases wonder. Through the compulsion which it exercises, it helps to define the channels of communication. Now philosophy and art likewise help to define the channels of communication, each by means of a distinctive mode of compulsion. Like science, they are concerned with whatever is discernible, though of course not in the same sense or in the same way. Like science, they make for understanding, and even for control—but again, for a very different kind of understanding and a very different kind of control.

Art is not evidentially compulsive. The notion of evidence is irrelevant because art is exhibitive and not assertive: the validation it seeks is open and unlimited, ever more determinate through the growth of reflexive and social communication. It is easy to suppose that in the light of such fundamental differences art is not compulsive at all; that its products, though they may emanate from the compulsiveness in individual invention, do not as products impose themselves with any demand on proception. Works of art are commonly regarded as gratuitous in a sense that theories are not. Theories presumably have a generic aim; works of art are individualistic, regionalistic, not subject to a governing discipline. They only await the process of deliberate assimilation, and they may reward it richly, but only with great diversity. And yet artistic invention and scientific invention are both gratuitous in this sense, at least: they are ultimately unregulated, unpredictable, and traceable to a proceptive direction and a communal atmosphere.

If the products of art are effective, they must be compulsive. Sociologically speaking, there is virtual unanimity in the gross evaluation of the influential products. Works of art filter through the clouds of discernment with a certain social and historical inevitability if chance can contrive to keep them in existence. Consensus in evaluation cannot be the result merely of fashion or of collusion. But suppose, even, that there is small agreement over the significance or merit of a work of art. The work will compel preference by some, and this compulsion will make it for them, first a work of art, and second, a satisfying work of art. In all cases, regardless of critical unanimity or diversity, there is a mode of compulsion distinctive of art as art. Art, science, and philosophy can be in part defined by the ways in which they compel, regardless of just how many human beings respond with approval or in a particular manner of approval. The enthusiast and the dissenter are compelled by a work of art to the extent that they see it as part of the artistic universe; and, likewise, the basis and character of their disagreement in philosophy will be in the philosophic mode. The product compels us not merely to classify and name but to augment, however negligibly, the materials of communication. The mode of controversy or criticism compelled by art is different from that compelled by science or philosophy. And this means that compulsion relates not merely to *acceptance* but to a kind of community and a kind of proceptive direction. We can be compelled, not necessarily to take, but to be.

The compulsiveness of an artistic product simply as such, independently of evaluative considerations, is perhaps best seen when the product is thought of not in so far as it emanates from query and is subject to direct scrutiny, but in so far as it is culturally localized and historically present. It is then seen to be an agent of its epoch. Since it holds the mirror up to the epoch as well as to nature, it is as compulsive as any other representation of the epoch. Historians appear much more inclined, though with doubtful justice, to stress the effect which economic and political institutions have on the individual than the effect which the art of his time has on him. Somehow it is supposed that he cannot be influenced in this direction unless he shows approval; yet a similar supposition in the case of social institutions would be absurd. The individual must breathe an air, but he may deem it foul. The art of a period need no more be thanked for its influence than the social institutions of that period.

Yet assimilation of a product of art can be characterized by assent, no less than that of a theory, and assent to the one can be compelled no less than assent to the other. We flatter ourselves too much on our power to give or withhold assent. It is more significant to see that both artistic and scientific assent admit of degrees. We say that some theories are better confirmed than others, and that a given theory is or is not confirmed to a sufficient degree. Similarly, we say that some works of art are more powerful, complex, or universal than others, and that a given work of art may grow in the degree of its acceptance. If the notion of degree of aesthetic acceptance seems to pose great difficulties for definition, it must be remembered that they are no greater than those involved in the definition of degree of confirmation. We are less tolerant of the development of taste in art than of the development of consensus in science: in art, curiously enough, we ascribe the slow growth of preference to the triumph of convention over compulsion, while in science it is precisely the slow growth of acceptance that we deem the mark of irresistible and inevitable cognitive force, the triumph of truth over special interests. In so far as it occurs either when products first emerge or when occasion arises to question established products, critical disputation in art is not fundamentally different from theoretical disputation in science. When specific products of art or science are seriously "revaluated," it is for good reasons. In art, cultural changes are indeed largely responsible; in science, intensified study and accumulation of observational data or the need for inter-theoretical connection. In both cases the lengthening of the heritage makes revision of perspective first possible and then necessary.

Assent to an exhibitive judgment is compelled both by its qualitative configuration and by the contingent circumstance of its relevancy to proceptive assimilation. Assent to a scientific theory is compelled not only by the character of its interpretation but by the predictive or deductive tie between the interpretation and the testimony of observation. This distinction is only another way of saying that exhibitive judgment is not evidentially compulsive. Now whether exhibitive judgment be considered as making or as not making an implicit cultural impression on one who is blind or deficient in power of assimilation, its compulsion is of one and the same kind. Science, we said, defines for the proceiver the relative limits of adaptive manipulation. His assent is a realization. If assent means direct realization (or conscious acceptance), then most men are compelled by the results of science and by the cultural trend of art without "assenting"; or, they assent only tacitly and indirectly. But there is something common to both instances of the compulsion: science defines the proceiver's manipulative limits *for* him; art affects his qualitative life and responses *for* him. Art compels by establishing only a different kind of realization in the proceiver. He comes either to sense or to utilize a qualitative modification in his relation to the work of art, or a qualitative gain in his proceptive direction. He responds not merely by satisfaction but by appropriating the product for the reflexive community. He understands more, not necessarily in the sense that he "learns more about himself" or that he grasps new "facts," but in the sense that the augmentation of his judgment widens his power of assimilation.

In the face of history, it would seem to be harder to speak of philosophic than of artistic compulsion. Philosophy is full of paradoxes. It probes and defines query at the same time that it is a form of query. It lays the basis for the most intimate sense of critical awareness by developing the most general of categories. It defines individuality and proception by aiming at the utmost in abstractness. It seeks to establish a perspective for the understanding of all forms of experience by relying upon a foundation of experience that is both antecedent and subsequent to all special forms. It interprets all human judgment not by transcending it but by systematically combining assertive and exhibitive judgments. Of all disciplines it is most exempt from the limitations of time and space, yet it is, of all disciplines, most self-conscious of its own history. With such enormous and exuberant latitude, how can it be said to be compelling?

Philosophy compels, not so much by the power of its individual judgments as by the character of its enterprise. If there is a sense in which the scientific method lives and thrives and develops by virtue of the theoretical devices that attack problems, there is a sense in which the reverse is true of the philosophic spirit, which is the miraculous source rather than the evolved product of special perspectives. Philosophy, like history, needs to be rewritten; not only because, as Dewey suggests, each age presents a special problem of interpretation, but because each age adds new matter to a continuous fund, new evidence to a continuous accumulation of evidence. Historical modifications of the philosophic idiom result not only from the birth of cultural idiosyncrasies but from the need to apply the heritage of foundational insights and distinctions. New cultures do raise new questions; but old questions need also to be retranslated for new cultures. Philosophy is not born anew in each age; it is the persistence of the philosophic spirit which compels the many perspectives of each age.

The compulsion of art, science, and philosophy lies in their effect on proception, not on a special faculty. When we say that art arouses a "sense of . . ." or that philosophy arouses a "sense of . . ." we are speaking of a proceptive modification rather than of a given type of feeling. "Realization," we suggested, is better than "sense": it avoids the implication of immediate or specific response. Philosophy effects a distinctive realization: that the categorial struggle to encompass structures of indefinitely greater breadth is both inevitable and valid. The philosopher comes to see that one perspective can excel or embrace but not annul another. Those who are most truly liberated by the philosophic spirit are likely to be most subject to the compulsion of other philosophies. Such compulsion does not entail literal cognitive acceptance but greater articulative mastery over one's own perspective and over the other, and greater conceptual endowment for the sense of encompassment.

Philosophers themselves have been much preoccupied with the circumstances of literal cognitive acceptance. That there are degrees of evidential compulsion it seems difficult to deny, even though (as in the case of other concepts where the factor of degree is involved) it may be more difficult to define the criterion by which these degrees are determined. Philosophers, however, have not been content to recognize degrees of evidential compulsion. They have sought judgments which embody a maximum or absolute of evidential compulsion, with a corollary distinction between kinds as well as degrees of compulsion. The appeal has most frequently been to "intuition" as the cognitive absolute, and the most recurrent distinction of levels has been that of intuitive, demonstrative, and sensitive knowledge. Just what is intuitively compulsive has been the stumbling block. Some philosophers have found their absolute in "self-evident" axioms or general principles; others, instead of contrasting the intuitive and the sensitive, have identified them, in the form of "common-sense" insights, or of sensations, or of perceptual judgments. Still others, like Locke, caught between the desire to preserve the threefold classification with its recognition of the inconclusiveness of sensory knowledge, and a distrust of systematic pretensions, compromised by conceiving of intuition as an elemental power of discrimination and by finding in "simple ideas" a compulsive content for knowledge.

Locke's notion of the "simple" (philosophers long before had been fascinated by the notion in one form or another) has had enormous influence on the subsequent history of empiricism and especially on recent British philosophy. The problem of "observational" or "atomic" or "basic" judgments —judgments known intuitively because they are compulsive and compulsive because they are "simple"—has been a subject of persistent controversy. There is some disagreement between those who regard such perceptual judgments as absolutely unalterable or incorrigible and those who regard them as only relatively incorrigible in their capacity as required instruments of verification in a given science. But what is common to these two groups of philosophers is the belief that both in the language of common discourse and in a science like psychology or physics there can be distinguished a class of judgments *simpler* than all the other judgments. By "simpler" they seem to mean "less corrigible than" or "more easily verifiable than." They assume (1) that these so-called basic judgments are less corrigible than judgments which are not basic, and (2) that one basic judgment cannot be said to have a greater or lesser degree of corrigibility than another. In the words of one philosopher: ". . . It is perhaps possible to think of expressions arranged in a *corrigibility-series:* we should begin with expressions that were highly *inferential,* and end with the 'direct record of experience' or protocol'"[7]—thus implying that perceptual judgments or protocols have all the same degree of simplicity or corrigibility.

But in the midst of the concern over the *existence* and *function* of basic judgments, no one seems to have bothered to establish the *identifying properties* of such judgments. By what standard can we recognize a judgment as "basic"?

Certain specifications seem to be discoverable from the way in which the notion has been used. The first is (*a*) that the judgment must be logically elementary, that is, it must contain no logical connectives such as "and" or "but." This specification is obviously insufficient, hence it appears (*b*) that if the assertion has the form $F(x)$ the values of x must be demonstrative symbols such as "I" or "this." But this too is insufficient, for no one regards "I am married" or "This is phanerogamous" as a basic judgment. It is accordingly sometimes held (*c*) that the predicate of the assertion must be "a simple adjective-name such as red,"[8] a "name of a simple quality," as the phrase usually goes. Just which names are "names of simple qualities" seems not to have troubled those who speak of basic judgments. They imagine it to be sufficiently clear to say "names *like* 'red.' "

Are the assertions "This is red" and "This is beige" both

"basic"? They have exactly the same form, but a great many people who are able to identify red are unable to identify or distinguish beige. The usual claim would be that once we acquaint ourselves with what the name "beige" denotes, we realize the two judgments to have the same corrigibility-status. A supposition made in this claim happens, first of all, to be contrary to fact: many people are unable to continue discriminating certain colors even after prior acquaintance. But more important is the fact that those who advance the claim presuppose a faculty of absolute recognition: once we perceive a quality, we can infallibly identify any perceptual recurrence of it. And this, in turn, means that we have the faculty of absolute feeling-comparison in memory, which, to say the least, is dubious. Notice, too, that the claim must abandon, in spite of itself, the distinction between simple and non-simple qualities. For all *felt* qualities are felt as "simple" in the sense that the experience of each is a distinctive whole. And if each feeling is always identifiable (that is, namable whenever recurrent), manifest differences in the corrigibility of demonstrative statements go by the board. It seems plain that "I see red" and "I feel depressed' can only with great difficulty be regarded as equally corrigible. But the absence of a satisfactory definition of "names of simple qualities" gives us no formal justification for discriminating the predicates "red" and "depressed."

Consider the predicates "hot," "lukewarm," and "barely warm." It will be generally acknowledged that what they denote is respectively more difficult to identify or distinguish accurately; that is to say, these predicates are respectively more difficult to apply. Assertions containing them might, perhaps, indifferently be called "observational judgments"; but are three such judgments basic in the same sense? And consider predicates relating to different sense-modalities. Are the visual predicate "red" and the kinaesthetic predicate "tense" alike "names of simple qualities"? It is at least open to doubt (and certainly most people would doubt) that even familiar judgments like "I see red," "I feel tense," "I smell cinnamon," and "I hear moaning" are always equally easy of verification; and that names for every one of the hundreds of odors, sounds, colors, textures, and tastes are equally easy of application. Those who speak of "names of simple qualities" or "names of qualities *like* red" cannot intend that such names should differ in the degree of applicability with which they are used. For with slight effort we might construct a hierarchy of names of qualities with increasing degrees of difficulty in application, and where shall we draw the line for the "names of simple qualities"? Those who have used this phrase to help define ultimately simple judgments have tacitly presupposed a certain psychological standard of familiarity, a standard which is variable and determined by all sorts of cultural or accidental considerations.

But not only is it true that judgments which have been called "basic" often have unequal degrees of corrigibility. It is also true that certain judgments not called "basic" have lesser degrees of corrigibility than those called "basic." On the view that basic judgments are demonstrative assertions about "simple" qualities, it should not be the case that judgments of a general character should be equally or more "certain." But is "I see red" more certain than "I see something"? The latter, clearly general, is equivalent to "There is an x which I see"; and I suggest that *it* is much less liable to error.

Some have pointed out that a class of observational statements may be interpreted either "phenomenologically" (as being about qualities "directly experienced") or "behavioristically" (as being about physical or publicly ascertainable properties). The foregoing examples have for the most part been "phenomenologically" interpreted. What about the question of relative corrigibility in a group of observational judgments interpreted in both ways? It is usually claimed that when "This is red" is "phenomenologically" understood, the judgment is less corrigible than when it is interpreted as the judgment about a physical property. Probably most people would agree. But I doubt that this is *always* true. For instance, I am not at all sure that we are less liable to erroneous judgment in "I *feel* tense" (a judgment purporting to identify the feeling) than in "I *am* tense" (a judgment purporting to identify the overt state).

And further: the frequency with which we correct ourselves when we judge "This is orange" or "This is red" is actually far greater than the frequency with which we correct ourselves when we make such assertions as "I live in North America" or "Sometimes it rains in New York" or "Ships cross the Atlantic Ocean." There *is* a sense in which it is easier to verify the former type of judgments, but there is unquestionably a sense in which the latter is more secure and compelling. There is nothing in the former which leads us to believe in quite the same way that there is in the latter. To contradict the former is in no way strange; to contradict the latter impresses us as ridiculous and artificial. Error in judgments about sensory qualities is common: special atmospheric or physiological conditions often are responsible for revision, and it is common practice to distrust sensory assertion even under presumed "standard" conditions. But error in the second type of judgment is militated against by the essential character of our social and biological existence, which supplies ramified evidence of an overpowering type. It is indeed true that the state of affairs designated is not investigable in "immediate experience"—on the contrary, the judgment is verified by so great a number, and so great a variety, of facts that it is impossible honestly to doubt it. Thus contradiction of the second type of judgment, unlike that of the first, will be belied by practice, by the commitments of the proceptive direction, and by the conditions of community.

Another type of assertion having a lesser degree of corrigibility than the perceptual judgment is the generalization of traditional experience: "Water quenches fire," "Summer days are longer than winter days." These generalizations are vague: they have scientific counterparts which qualify and abstract. But it is as a result of this very vagueness that the reference of the statements forms so intimate a part of common experience. "Water" for common experience is not a chemical term but the name of a pervasive qualitative phenomenon. So that here again the truth of the judgment is based not, as that of the perceptual judgment is, on single and very fallible identifications but on a manifold social confirmation.

One current view which regards basic judgments as constituting a special class but lays down no identifying properties beyond those we have considered is an exception, however, because it regards basic judgments as differing from other factual assertions in kind rather than in degree (of corrigibility). A contemporary writer says: "If I say 'I am in pain' or 'This is red' I may be lying, or I may be using words wrongly; that is, I may be classifying as 'pain' or as 'red' something that would not normally be so classified. But I cannot be mistaken in any other way. I cannot be mistaken in the way that I can be mistaken if I take this red patch to be the cover of a book. If this is a fact, it is not a fact about human psychology. . . . It is, if anything, a fact about language."[9]

Thus presumably when we judge "This is red" we can be mistaken only in the sense that we are using words "wrongly." But is not this precisely what our being mistaken in the assertion of *any other* judgment consists in? To be mistaken is to use words which fail in some way to characterize the situation referred to. In saying that an assertion is corrigible we mean that it contains terms which may turn out to be descriptively inadequate. And it is in this sense that the words of an assertion which is mistaken are used "wrongly." In the very same way, to be mistaken in judging a thing to have the color red or myself to be in pain is to use a word that is descriptively inadequate. (To judge that we are in pain when we are merely in the state of expecting pain is a common situation. There is always *some* feeling which we have when we make such a judgment, but we must remember not to confuse the feeling with the assertion. It is not feelings which are mistaken.) When we call beige "ivory" we are inadequately describing beige, just as we inadequately describe a red patch when we call it "cover of a book."

If the view just examined is not (as it seems to be) confused, if it intends something entirely different, it must be that we have a power of identifying certain qualities absolutely, and that in being mistaken when describing them we are only using a word inadvertently—the "wrong" word. This involves the dubious notion of absolute recognizability. But worse, if there are absolutely recognizable qualities, which qualities are they, and how are they to be distinguished from those which are not absolutely recognizable? If we can infallibly identify red as a property of a thing, and accordingly assign the name, why can we not infallibly identify cover-of-a-book as the property of a thing, and accordingly assign the name, since each perception, after all, is a distinctive qualitative whole?

Thus it appears that although within rough limits we can differentiate degrees of corrigibility, no satisfactory measure of corrigibility has been defined, and no standard of uniform corrigibility for a class of absolutely simple judgments has been

established. The discrimination of basic from non-basic predicates, in such a way as to insure that a class of judgments containing the basic predicates fulfills conditions (1) and (2), is
not achieved by the criterion consisting of provisions (*a*),
(*b*), and (*c*).[10]

IV
CONVENTION

WE CAN SPEAK OF COMPULSION in connection with both procepts and products, but of convention only in connection with products. Compulsion and convention are predicable of one and the same judgment, but only in so far as its relationships differ. Compulsion obtains where a judgment cannot be regarded as determined by decision; convention, in any other case—that is, in so far as a judgment can be regarded as determined by decision. The same judgment can be compulsive when considered as part of one order and conventional when considered as part of another. Hence, of any judgment we can say that it is either compulsive or conventional, but we cannot thereby mean that it is absolutely or unqualifiedly one or the other. And I shall suggest that any human product can be shown to function in these two dimensions; or, if we would formulate it differently, to be located in at least two orders, one of which shows it to be compulsive and the other conventional.

In common usage we attach the notion of convention to those practices or beliefs which are tacitly agreed upon and not explicitly justified. A convention is something accepted without question and even with relative willingness, though in fact alterable. Thus we speak of the conventions of the theatre, the conventions of parliamentary procedure, the conventions of apparel.

"Convention" here carries a dual suggestion: partly that of "convening" and partly that of "convenience." The convention is a result of convening in so far as it represents a heritage of assent. It is, as it were, a perpetuation and hardening of some vaguely established social contract. But whether the source of a convention is social or proceptive is a matter of history only: the idea of convening can be generalized to include the reflexive community. Voluntary choices, however they may be compelled by the proceptive direction, are the results of query, and query is one kind of convening. The conventions of social practice are usually acknowledged to be dispensable, in the sense that without a given convention the social human can remain both social and human; and yet, paradoxically, they are often accompanied by tyrannical sanctions. When we are told that it is best not to depart from convention, we are being confronted by the persistent voice of the social contract, the original convening, and hence of course with a moral pronouncement about the desirability of retaining a connection with the past. The order which we abandon when we abandon a social convention of this type—we may call such a convention a consanction —coincides with some community.

Some conventions are the result of transmission or habituation, others are the result of resolution or special contrivance; conventions, in other words, are accepted or devised. The use of a national language is a convention of the former type, the styling of fashions in clothes is of the latter type. Conventions of habituation are not necessarily of social origin: it is my proceptive direction, not my cultural group, that transmits to the present moment my custom of walking down the street with my hands in my pockets. When I decide to walk with hands free I am introducing a convention by resolution no less than when I decide to give a name to my cat. It is in the devised conventions rather than in the accepted conventions that the element of "convenience" assumes equal importance with the element of convening. When a dramatist decides to adopt new theatrical "conventions," he is choosing to employ devices which are expedients because they are minor means to a major end. He trusts that in the community of his theatre a new social contract will take place whereby his artistic conveniences will become spectatorial conveniences. What are commonly regarded as the conventions of query in art, philosophy, and science, for instance choices in sensuous media or in nomenclature, are frequently devices to facilitate communication, and are in this sense expedients. This does not mean that the promotion of communication is necessarily subordinate to invention; on the contrary, it could be said to be the final cause of all judgment. But it is often the case that although one alternative is superior in facilitating communication, any of the alternatives has the same ultimate influence in communication. And it may also be the case that the choice of a convention means a choice based on "convenience" in some particular respect, so far as a number of alternatives is concerned. The element of convenience may be biographical, physical, or of some other kind genuinely extrinsic to the burden of judgment. On the non-formal level—and even to a certain extent on the formal—human judgment utilizes accepted and devised conventions (habits and resolutions) in inextricable compounds. In all utterance, and very plainly in that type of utterance which we commonly know as discourse, we oscillate between customary and unique judgments. Every unique product occurs in a recognizable or customary context, and every such context is a sub-context of a uniquely ordered product. Thus even the most arbitrary nomenclature must be embedded in a commonly assimilable structure if continuity of communication, reflexive or social, is to be preserved.

It is evident that what are designated as "conventions" in common usage, being products of proception or communication, are active, assertive, or exhibitive judgments. The conventions of etiquette or of theatrical performance may be regarded as active judgments in so far as they are ways of behaving, and as exhibitive judgments in so far as they are ways of ordering and shaping materials. In the same way, conventions of moral conformity or of legal procedure, and perhaps consanctions in general, may be regarded as active or assertive in accordance with whether they are to be regarded as established ritual or as claims to truth. Now there is a more limited usage of the term "convention" according to which we regard it as a "convention" to suppose that the pen which I am now using does not change its size when I write with it. Here the suggestion is that while theoretically we could ascertain whether this is or is not the case, we find it unquestionably more convenient to suppose that it is not, because there "is no reason" to change such a supposition. Such a convention is regarded as an assertive judgment which is inconsequential or of negligible importance methodologically. But there is another usage according to which, for instance, we "conventionally" assume that all our measuring instruments retain their size or structure when we employ them in measuring. Here the convention is not currently regarded as an assertion, since by the very circumstances we assume, it is neither verifiable nor refutable. It is of a different genus—a "rule," a "policy." A rule or policy of this kind can be regarded as an active judgment: we choose not to speak in such and such a way, not to use symbols that would make it seem as if we entertained a problem which we do not entertain. Such a convention, therefore, would have the same status as that by which we agree to employ a certain configuration of symbols as a name for such and such a complex.

Consider now one further type of convention in the methodology of natural science. In the process of confirmation our technique of measurement may yield results which, applied to the same phenomenon, vary. We determine a range within which the values of the measurement fall, and we select one quantity, "conventionally," as representative of the experimental decision. Or consider a process of confirmation which depends on sampling the presence of a certain property in an indefinite number of complexes. Since the number is indefinite, we determine "conventionally" when (or with which instance) the confirmation may be deemed established. What seems to be fundamental here is not so much the factor of "convenience," for it might be no less convenient to continue further in each case, but rather a factor of indifference. The convention is an expression of indifference so far as confirmation is concerned; that is, further experimentation is declared to be irrelevant to the character of the goal in question. And the same factor is present in the other commonly accepted instances of convention: it is indifferent to the process of measurement whether or not we suppose our instruments to vary when not in use; it is indifferent to my practical and intellectual life whether I suppose the size of my pen to remain constant or not; it is indifferent to the content of a given science, after a certain stage in its development, whether some of its judgments are established as "laws" or as "definitions." It is presumably indifferent to the functioning of a drama whether we choose one alternative or another as a staging device; or to the basic affairs of mankind whether we are accustomed to one kind of attire or another; or to the issues of discussion whether we choose one set of parliamentary regulations or another.

Convention, then, is the measure of indifference in proception and communication. "Indifference," of course, is to be taken in a very literal sense and stripped of its usual emotional connotation. The proceptive process contains points or stations at which latitude of judgment occurs. These are, so to speak, proceptive variables. But latitude is always relative latitude: judgments can be conventional only in a given respect and to a given extent. A judgment is conventional with respect to a given end if its replacement by some other judgment will not influence or alter the character of that end. What I mumble to my next-door neighbor of a morning could be replaced by something else without influencing the character of our relations as neighbors. The first sentence of a book might be altered without affecting the burden or the public reception of the book. It might be that my saying anything other than what I do say or using any other sentence than the one I do use would disturb my own comfort or equanimity, and hence the judgment in question would not be conventional in this respect even though it would be in the former. For in this respect the judgment would be compulsive as the means to the particular end involved. To say that one judgment may replace another without influencing the character of a given end is not to deny that the means always influences the end. If the latter notion makes any sense at all, it must be that the end is influenced by the character of a means and not by each and every particular instance of that character.

Similarly, consanctions are practices or principles not devoid of significance but rather indifferently exchangeable with alternative practices and principles as devices for social regulation. Some principles may be of lesser "convenience" to individuals or groups, yet the end which they subserve may be indifferently achieved. Some types of nomenclature or some types of sensuous representation may be more convenient in the ordinary processes of manipulation, but both the more and the less convenient may function equally as instruments of assertive or exhibitive content.

A judgment, we said, is conventional to a given extent as well as in a given respect. I can replace the words to my neighbor, but not by any words; nor can I begin a book with a sentence at random. The conventional choice is limited to judgments of a certain class. The extent of the convention, the degree of its latitude, is definable in terms of a type. A musical phrase may be replaced by many other phrases, but by phrases of a specifiable character, depending on the order (perspective, context)* under consideration. A numerical value assigned to an algebraic variable may be one of an infinite set of possible choices, but it must be a numerical symbol and not any symbol. A convention for which there would be a maximum of latitude, which could be replaced by any other judgment within a given order, would be an arbitrary convention. The protestations of a prisoner in solitary confinement could perhaps be regarded as arbitrary judgments—but, even as arbitrary, the qualification that they relate to an order is necessary, for in the proceptive domain of the prisoner they may be tragically compulsive. Given a specified order, then, a judgment for which any other judgment is substitutable without altering the character of what remains in the order is an arbitrary convention. I am asked to devise a new game for the entertainment of youngsters. I define a context to guide me: that the game be playable indoors, that the rules be intelligible and capable of retention by an average memory, and that they exclude violence. Within this context the number of possible rules is indefinite and my selection is arbitrary. But arbitrariness with respect to the origination of the game may not be arbitrariness with respect to its survival. The rules that determine a game yield

* For further clarification of these terms, please see Appendix.

the qualities of just that game and no other; so that in a context defined by the requirement that the game be desired and that it sustain interest, the degree of conventional latitude may shrink, away from arbitrariness and into a relatively narrow area of choice.

An order for any convention is always specifiable, but it may be extremely difficult to determine; and the same is true of the degree of conventional latitude. In other words, it is possible to know or to define the character of a context without being able to enumerate all the criteria for location within the context. Any one defining characteristic may have an indefinite number of consequences not all of which can be previsioned. Thus, perhaps, the constituent judgments of art, considered as individual, are more likely to have a conventional character relative to the artistic judgments with which they are associated than are the judgments of science; yet in the former the determination of context and degree, even the selection of context and degree, is more elusive and problematical than in the latter.

Although every judgment can be conventional only in relation to some context within which it is conventional, a distinction is necessary between conventions which are independent of all other judgments in a context, or dependent only upon a specific number in that context, and conventions which are inseparable from an indefinite number of other judgments in a context. We may call the former loose conventions, the latter ramified conventions. My morning greeting is replaceable without replacing all the other, or even any of the other, judgments my neighbor and I make about each other.

It is a loose convention (though not an arbitrary one). Consider, however, the judgment that what I see before me is a "sense-datum" with the qualities of squareness and whiteness. This judgment is a convention replaceable by the assumption that there are no sense-data before me at all but that the squareness and whiteness are qualities of what I call a piece of paper, qualities which belong to the paper under certain conditions, one of which is my visual perspective. Either of these judgments indifferently effects a description; neither influences in the least the qualities which I mention. But if I adopt either one of them, I am committed to an indefinite number of judgments based on the assumption involved or in some other way associated with it. Either "language" commits me to an entire "philosophy." The entire language apparatus can be regarded as conventional, for I can substitute the other language without altering my selection and description of the qualities involved. Either of the two assumptions is conventional so far as my choice is concerned, but compulsive so far as my commitment to an entire class of judgments is concerned. Both are ramified conventions. But what are loose conventions in one context may be ramified in another, and vice versa.

I have suggested thus far that a judgment is conventional to the extent that its selection is not more of a determining factor in the character of a given context than is that of some alternative to it. The conventionality is a property of the product, not of the intentions of the producer. But at the beginning of this chapter a much wider claim seemed to have been made, namely,

that any product which can be regarded as determined by decision is conventional. The one criterion
seems to be that the conventionality of a product depends upon its status of relative indifference within a
context; the other, that the conventionality of a product
depends upon the interpretation of its origin as due to
decision. If these two criteria are to coincide, as I believe they do, it must be shown that in so far as a product is due to decision it is relatively indifferent with
respect to the character of some context.

Now by a decision we can only mean a selection from
alternatives. And if the selection is genuinely a selection
and not just an act without alternatives, there must
be some margin of indifference in it. One choice, as
compared with another, may indeed have vastly different consequences, or may be revoked and negated. But
relative to that basic context which consists in the sheer
adoption of a means to an end, any judgment is conventional. That is to say, either of the alternative judgments equally well satisfies the requirement of *serving
as* an answer, a tool, a means. The subsequent fate, the
inherent content of an answer is another matter. Sub-
stantiating or evaluating an answer can be regarded as
one context, adopting or selecting an answer can be regarded as another.

The best way to envisage the conventional character
of all decision is to think of those cases in which
query, active, exhibitive, or assertive, is begun and
is completed. How shall we begin to do or make or say
anything? We must begin. No matter what the restriction, there are different or alternative ways to begin.

Any one of a number of judgments can inaugurate a complex judgment; any one out of a number can serve; all are indifferent so far as the sheer inauguration is concerned. However delicate the moral transaction which we undertake, however momentous the work of art or the theoretical enterprise, there is a margin of indifference, an inescapable fortuity in the genesis. The same is true of the completion. When shall a moral situation, an artistic enterprise, a process of verification be regarded as consummated? In each instance, with the progressive articulation of the product the scope of the compulsions involved becomes narrower. In each instance the termination is eventually accomplished by resolution: we decide, we feel, we suspect that this or that should be the end. For we pass the stage where a moral, an artistic, an evidential compulsion precludes resolutions. What is the signal that the product is "complete"? Moral "conscience," aesthetic "intuition," theoretical "belief" are simply labels for the actual circumstances of resolution. We can, of course, envision the act of termination in judgment as compulsive in one way or another; but this is not to deny, or is only another way of recognizing, that where the termination is seen as a decision it is conventional or indifferent qua termination.

What is true of the genesis and the consummation of a product is seen upon reflection to be true of any phase of it. Each phase of a product is a product. Each is a miniature genesis and consummation. Each "individual" judgment, as a selection from alternatives, is indifferent relative to *some* specifiable context. A decision is a leap. It may of course be the covert expression of a habit of thinking or doing, or the covert application of a rule. But even by thus exhibiting a compulsion involved, we would not be settling the rationale of the decision. The decision itself is a guess with respect to its own rationale.

In spite of the fact that every product can be regarded, in some order, as a conventional determination, it seems clear that there are degrees of latitude in decision. Difficult as it may often be to discriminate such degrees with precision, or to specify criteria for discrimination, I suspect it would be universally conceded that in some sense we can consider the choice of specific foods as allowing greater latitude than the choice of food as such, or the choice of scientific notation as allowing greater latitude than the choice of natural traits in a given description. It is always possible to specify the kind of consideration in virtue of which we exercise a latitude. But to what extent is it significant to ask, for instance, how latitude of choice in artistic creation compares with that in scientific investigation?

Having known a piano sonata by Beethoven, we may not wish a single note to be otherwise; yet it is not difficult to suppose that if certain constituents had been different the result might have been equally impressive, or indifferent to an appraisal of the whole. The margin of latitude, the range within which variation is allowable, is measurable by many different standards—that of the composer's proceptive direction, or of his floating proceptive domain in some circumstance; that of a given auditor; or that of a society of habituated auditors. Given an exhibitive judgment of a certain genus, the conventional latitude for its constituent judgments is in large part predetermined: we could not, for example, indifferently accept a passage of ancient Hindu music as desirable anywhere at all in the Beethoven sonata, nor a passage of the sonata as desirable anywhere in the music for Martha Graham's choreography, nor an unplaned piece of pine lumber as one of the four legs in a mahogany chair. Our habits of aesthetic expectation, the crystallization and rationalization of our preferences establish the general framework within which the types of latitude in artistic utterance are determined.

There is no doubt that, in the major intellectual and popular climate of western culture, science is not pictured as allowing the same kind of latitude in judgment. The supposition that naturally springs from a technologically influenced society is that art is less remote and more available to lay comprehension. Even when art forms are declared unintelligible, this hardly stands in the way of confident disapproval. The result of this assumption that lay judgment has greater authority in art than it has in science is that art is deemed psychologically and morally more dispensable than science. A more serious basis for the contention that science is generically different from art so far as the latitude of its choices is concerned, is the presence in the former of evidential and formal compulsion, or the compulsive demands of fact and logic. Aesthetic compulsion, whether on the productive or on the assimilative level, might be regarded as "personal," that of fact and logic as "impersonal." But in rebuttal it can be contended that the patterns of human demand and of human expectation are no less refractory, no less "natural" or ontologically "given" than the patterns of fact and logic. And it can be further argued, conversely, that the scientific fabric of judgment is a conceptual instrument devised by men to discover the compulsion of evidence and of consistency; that even the most general or central hypotheses can be imagined to have been different in varying degrees; and that what we cannot help regarding as the indispensable or conclusive character of the present scientific structure reflects after all only a retrospective attitude based on the feeling that what has actually emerged from scientific thinking is nothing less than the best under the historical circumstances.

Nothing in the nature of discourse, action, or contrivance can fix boundaries for latitude of decision. In the last analysis the conditions of such latitude lie in the proceptive direction or in the bases of community. It is of the greatest importance not to understand this statement as implying that latitude of decision "depends upon" factors of a "subjective" or "personal" or "sociological" character; so to understand it would be to misunderstand the concepts of community and proceptive direction. The proceptive direction cannot be dissociated from the nature of the procepts that go to shape and determine it or that become phases of it. To look upon latitude of decision—and upon convention in general—as ultimately functional expressions of proception and community is therefore to emphasize rather than to overlook the compulsive framework which natural complexes impose and within which latitude becomes latitude.

The nature of conventional latitude constitutes additional evidence of the relative fluidity of inquiry, of art, and of moral conduct, and additional evidence against faith in finally determinate rules, imperatives, and canons. In all judgment there is residual randomness, and this randomness reflects what we earlier distinguished as proceptive drift. Neither in molding nor in assimilating a product can we guarantee antecedently just where we shall deem its alterable or dispensable ingredients to lie; the context of a specific randomness is indeterminate. Nor can we ascertain with lasting rigor or in any instance how great the margin of randomness will be. For the proceptive direction and the bonds of community are themselves in process and fluctuate irregularly. It is on proceptive latitude—on the blind grace of one natural force embedded in others —that the degrees of conventional latitude depend.

In what sense is the philosopher's selection of categories conventional? The answer depends on how we interpret the philosophic enterprise. As the modern divergence between philosophy and the special sciences has increased, the inclination of most laymen and of many philosophers has been to regard philosophy as fictitious in a sense in which science never could be. Philosophy has been seen as personal, science as social. The philosopher is seen as inventing categories in response to his own ingenious vision, even as gratifying narcissistic impulses toward self-expression, while the scientist is seen as responding to nature's demand for articulation. The philosopher accentuates and exaggerates the traits of existence that appeal to his sense of significance; the scientist immerses his private perspective in the selfless, the merciless process of explanation.

Such a view will almost surely lay emphasis upon philosophic categories as "conventional," and will perhaps even fall prey to the elementary if common confusion of the conventional and the arbitrary; but paradoxically enough, it will usually emphasize the importance of philosophic "vision." Presumably the selection of categories is a matter of relative indifference; the crux of the matter is, how great an impact can the result of philosophizing make on the human imagination? The analogy here, whether consciously supposed or not, is with art: the choice of materials, the means, is evaluated entirely in terms of the character of the product. From this point of view it is the philosopher's manipulative skill rather than the type of his conceptions that makes his vision humanly impressive.

When philosophy is interpreted rather as reflecting the traits of a culture—when it is seen, with Dewey for example, as a "conversion of culture into consciousness" —its categories can hardly be regarded as conventional in the same sense. For philosophic thinking is seen as reacting to or reflecting something, specifically the presuppositions and values and ideals of an age. Hence even contrasting philosophies are rendered intelligible by historical and social circumstances. And what becomes important in the philosophic enterprise is not so much the constructive imagination as the expressive content of the categories. Categories can be artificial but not accidental or conventional. The conventional factor is placed in terminology, idiom, and degree of eloquence.

Philosophers have often regarded the conventional as in some sense the fictional. It is that which is primarily the product of contrivance as opposed to that which is primarily the product of description or delineation. Conventions are seen as necessary evils, useful fictions as against misleading or false fictions, devices required for the conduct of life, for practical accommodation and successful adaptation. It is no accident that many philosophers have looked at art or the life of contrivance as make-believe, as imagination in the sense of "fancy," as the fictitious descent into the realm of sensuous delight, to be severed by stern vigilance from the contemplative realm of the understanding. And it is no accident that the reaction to this has been primarily an extreme reaction, turning the tables and making art the realm of a deeper understanding, a deeper insight into reality, an escape from what is rather held to be the fictions or conventions of ordinary human discourse. The conventional, then, has been one name for what philosophers have deemed appearance as contrasted with reality. It is a covert term of evaluation, applied to that which is of lesser importance morally or methodologically in the domain of human knowledge or human action.

In this manner almost every fundamental phase of

life and existence known to man has been relegated by one school or another to the status of the conventional: sense-perception, art, science, religion, language, abstract ideas, theories, political institutions. "By convention there is sweet; by convention, bitter; by convention, hot; by convention, cold; by convention, colour; but in truth there exist atoms and the void." Here the conventional is the socially indispensable and the metaphysically dispensable. It is the judgment influenced by custom and human expediency—the socially easy and the proceptively expedient version of cognition. It is truth by convenience, but less than truth because irrelevant to explanation and prediction. The convention lies in the decision to emphasize the derived and to remain indifferent to the underlying, the primary. The convention of description is also a convention of action: the cognitive conventions support the moral conventions whereby the shocking impact of the implacable world of particles in empty space is circumvented. The compulsion to which men are ultimately subject is mitigated by being sensuously dressed.

Hobbes and Locke could adhere to the mechanical universe of Democritus as the substructure of compulsion and hence of truth, but they questioned the conceptual price of recognizing it. Hobbes loved system, but because he distrusted abstract ideas he reduced it to calculation based on verbal agreement. Locke distrusted system as well as abstract ideas, and saw sense-perception not as the barrier to, but as the avenue of compulsion. Abstractions were both dangerous and useful. They were dangerous because they opened the way to symbols without content. They were useful as ways of representing masses of particulars. They would be superfluous to gods who could make direct contact with such particulars; for men they are conventions, in principle dispensable, but profitable as a compromise with the limitations which nature has imposed on the race.

In more recent times conventional status has come to be assigned not merely to abstract ideas but to abstract generalization or theory. The fact of constantly altering interpretations in science and in politics has engendered at least two important conventionalistic attitudes toward the status of theory. One regards theory as a static or frozen account of what in the concrete is either unique and evolving or too rich in content to be merely described. The other regards it as a technique or tool for organizing discrete percepts and for introducing predictability and coherence into a mute flux. Both views regard theory as not primarily a vehicle of "truth," but for very different and even opposite reasons. The first, because theory is essentially a partial and distorting agency; the second, because "truth" is only an inaccurate and vague concept vitiated by the suggestion of eternal and immutable doctrine. Both views see theory as secondary, but again in very different senses and for very different reasons. The one, because there is a way of knowing superior to theory; the other, because theory is under the cognitive obligation of accommodating itself to a fund of insistent sensory materials. Both views see theory as largely conventional because of the great role played in it by language and by symbolic devices. But the first interprets this conventionality in terms of practical convenience and assumes that it is the price paid for preferring symbolic or discursive analysis to "immediate" insight; the second regards the conventionality of theory as consisting in the fact that symbolically ordered devices can achieve knowledge in an indefinite number of ways or formulations.

Whatever the respective difficulties in these views, they have certain limitations in common. They fail to make clear the complementarity as well as the exhaustiveness of compulsion and convention in human inquiry. They fail also to understand the pervasiveness of compulsion and convention, their role and presence not merely in inquiry but in the omnipresent process of utterance, in active and exhibitive as well as in assertive judgment. Both are inclined to look upon convention as a compensatory implement of one kind or another in the relation of man to nature, rather than as a natural dimension of human utterance. And both fail to discern the relative character of convention: they look for it in this or that area of judgment rather than in the contextual circumstances of judgment.

The notion of convention assumes dramatic significance when we apply to any human judgment the question, What if it were otherwise? The accidents underlying human choice and the accidental perspectives in which it is made seem to cast doubt on the preferability of any judgment to its alternatives. No one with a minimum of self-consciousness fails to question from time to time the desirability, the force, or the soundness of certain of his major utterances. To question the entire basis of one's utterances is another matter. Verbally we can admit as plausible the idea that the method or predilection which underlies our preferences is a mere ripple, a neutral and unique event among countless events in nature. To accept this as a living datum would mean the stultification of judgment and hence of the proceptive direction. A universal conventionalism of this kind would see all judgment as a local peculiarity and all compulsion as only an indiscriminate causal sequence or fact of nature. It would be far more radical than the traditional skepticisms; for Hume and the Pyrrhonists are impressed not by the ultimate indifference of all judgments but by the much more limited problem of cognitive uncertainty. It would even transcend ancient philosophic nihilism, which questioned all claims of knowing without discerning the implied, equally questionable status of human utterance in any form.

It is undeniable that the judgments of man are facts of nature in the very same sense that the falling of snowflakes and the orbits of the planets are. But from this it hardly follows that there is no qualitative difference among such facts. Similarly, all human judgments are judgments in the same sense; but from this, likewise, it does not follow that all judgments can be regarded as indiscriminately acceptable or valuationally equal. We may appreciate the likeness without overlooking the difference. The opponents of naturalism have often been guilty of the confusion in their assumption that naturalistic ethics renders all moral judgments indifferent.

Variety in fact and hierarchy in estimation and preference are themselves facts of nature, natural complexes.
A critical naturalism, of all philosophic perspectives, is
the one from which such facts can never be omitted.

To reveal the conventional element in human judgments is not to abolish the indefinitely numerous bases of
distinction among them. Any scientific hypothesis is
conventional in the sense that it cannot be regarded as
the only possible hypothesis under the circumstances
which evoke it. But its explanatory success is in no way
diminished by this realization. "Convention" still carries
a pejorative overtone, accompanied by a gracious con-
cession that it has some utility. We do not like to
think of our products as conventions because we do not
like to think of our acts and opinions as alterable. This
latent fear is a subtle carry-over from classical rationalism, which has so far influenced our cultural orientation that we look upon the ideal of all judgment as ir-
revocability. To find convention in works of art or in
philosophic principles is allegedly to find products devoid of power and producers unable to discern the testa-
ment inherent in the nature of things.

V
PERSPECTIVE

IF WE CONCEIVED OF JUDGMENTS as though they were units the sum of which constitute the productive life of man, we would be thinking not erroneously so much as elliptically. A judgment reflects something larger than itself, by virtue of which indeed it is the judgment that it is and has the meaning or communicative effect that it has. The larger framework is commonly called a "point of view," but we may use the somewhat more economical and more general term "perspective." It must be clear from the outset that a perspective is the essence of a judgment, the condition and the potentiality of its completion, rather than a psychological aspect of it or a historical circumstance explaining its occurrence. Whenever we explain the purpose of what we are doing (as in active and exhibitive products) or the purport of what we are saying in our assertions, we are helping to supply, and even to discover, the perspective of a judgment. A perspective is as much part of the content and of the "language" or material of a judgment as the so-called direct ingredients.

The properties ordinarily ascribed to judgment— for instance, meaning, truth, moral value, or social influence—belong to it only in virtue of some perspective which it represents. I say *some* perspective, because, first, a judgment may represent more than one perspective; and second, a property assignable to judgment belongs to it in virtue of some one, but not necessarily all, of the perspectives that it represents. For example "2 + 2 = 4" belongs to a perspective commonly known as the system of arithmetic, but it may also function in the perspective of my own reflection on numbers. In the former, the judgment has the properties of meaning and truth; in the latter, it may also have the property of aesthetic significance. This property may be thought irrelevant in the one perspective and indispensable in the other. The active judgment which consists in the theft of a wallet will relate to the perspective of a social code, and to the various perspectives identified with anyone who is either involved in the act or for whom it is a procept. To say that a judgment is present in different perspectives is to say that it is related to each of them, or is a product of each, in a distinctive respect. A judgment, like any other natural entity or event, functions in different settings and under different conditions. And what applies to judgments applies to procepts. If procepts could not to some extent be similar as well as unique for different proceivers, communication would not be possible. A storm is a procept for five residents each at a different distance from it. It is the same storm for all five, though unique for each in its intensity. The one event, assimilated and identified by all, would not (and indeed could not) have the same total properties for all.

Perspectives, then, can be shared by different proceivers, just as objects can (though not *all* perspectives are sharable), and community of perspective is as essential for communication as common availability of objects. When we say that the same object is a procept for different proceivers, we mean that they share at least one perspective: they judge or "see" in the same respect; in that respect they are a distinctive community. On the other hand, men cannot have all perspectives in common, for this would mean that each had the same proceptive direction as every other, and this in turn would mean, by the analysis of what an individual is, that there is only one individual. There will always be some philosophers to whom such a conclusion is metaphysically congenial, however deft must be the means by which it is reached.

Perspectives can include or comprehend other perspectives. For each individual the widest perspective is the proceptive domain. The imminent and the floating domain are perspectives which define the individual's life, while the indefinitely numerous perspectives describable within these domains define that life's interests. The perspectives in a man's life can be related concentrically as it were; but they also are parallel, they intersect, they are of commensurable and incommensurable, of variable and invariable types.

Every conflict known to history, whether political, military, economic or ideational, has been a conflict of perspectives. This does not mean that combatants share no perspective, or that opposition is solely a matter of misunderstanding. The absence of any values or aims in common means blind collision, not opposition. Combatants understand each other precisely to the extent that they share some perspective. Their conflict lies in the character that belongs to the total interrelation of the perspectives of each, and in the moral quality of the community involved. In some phases of human experience opposition can occur only where prior community is dominant community rather than circumstantial togetherness. Thus controversy in natural science implies an effort by each side to extend the dominant community to an area where it does not yet obtain. The kind of achievement in which the solution of a problem consists is in large part the achievement of a common perspective. Philosophic controversy rests on a smaller community of perspective, and either on a lesser willingness to achieve community or on a different conception of what community entails.

But the existence of misunderstanding must not be underestimated. History written in terms of rejections and acceptances by the parties to conflict exaggerates rational awareness of alternative perspectives and rational discrimination among them. If fanaticism entails unreasonable blindness, simple opposition often entails unwitting blindness. To be sure, the realization that other perspectives are perspectives hardly insures community. Perspectives can be rejected most emphatically when they are best understood. But when disagreement is based on knowledge of what such disagreement implies, that is, when it is based on deliberately achieved community of perspective, conflict becomes controversy and human opposition is *ipso facto* in its rational phase. Rationality could be defined as the willingness to discover other perspectives, to attain community of perspective, and to reconcile community with conviction.

Not only may perspectives be shared; they may be adopted, though adoption itself takes place within the framework of another perspective. Adoption of a perspective may be the result of compulsion or convention. At one extreme, catastrophic events may force a radically different perspective into being; at the other, a perspective may be replaced as a means to intellectual economy, with relatively little change in the character of thought or in the proceptive direction.

Perspectives are more than conditions of life and judgment. They underlie moral ideals and they can be direct objects of moral preference. Political legislation and moral analysis are ways in which men fix perspectives. The enactment of a statute is the definition of a framework for conduct. Every valuation is not only the choice of a perspective but the recommendation of it as persistent and habitual, as a proceptive pattern. Moral disagreement, like all disagreement, can stem from mutual ignorance of the perspectival conditions of judgment; but it can stem as often and perhaps more often from proceptive repugnance and incapacity, and from the sheer accidents that determine man's lot on earth. Though perspectives are adoptable, the most influential and fundamental of them are, so far as the intercourse of men is concerned, rarely held by a simple act of choice. They coalesce with the proceptive direction by the junction of many factors—the chances of the world, the powers of the social community, the flexibility of the proceiver, the nature and limits of all proceivers. Moral perspectives are among the least mobile, proceptively speaking. The guiding moral tone of the individual is the attribute least visible to him and least isolable by him.

Difference of perspective, we said, is as fundamental to communication as the sharing of perspective. Men communicate by interrogative and positive judgment, by laboring to transform and concretize interrogation into manageable questions, and affirmation into plausible answers. Whatever their social or grammatical guise, some products question, others propose. A shared perspective is the means by which questions take form; cross-perspectives are the means by which answers are developed. Good questions depend upon common answers and effect diverse answers. Difference of perspective saves query from sterility and inanity. But the character of a perspective is as important as its identity, and it can lend itself to idolatry as well as to exploration. The great faiths of men, the great "schools" of philosophy and art, have been the influential perspectives within which men have been able to attain coherency. They have functioned as quasi-social devices by which query has defined its order and within which it has fed itself. They have also been castles of orthodoxy. Their borders have hardened into impassable fortresses, and the processes of query have dried into vested interests of the spirit. Some perspectives, some communities are porous; others are opaque, as brittle as they are dark. At first blush it would seem that by definition all perspectives are in some sense opaque, but there is a difference between opaqueness and distinctiveness.

Although the meaning of every judgment depends

on the perspective within which it functions as a judgment, it does not follow that to render explicit the
perspective of a judgment always is one and the same
type of process. The disciplines of man vary consider-
ably with respect to the kinds of perspective which play
a role in them. Thus physics and history may be said
to employ the generic perspective of science in the
technique of their query. But within the subject matter
of physics a special kind of perspective, the frame of
reference, is explicitly recognized and is indispensable
for the meaning of certain judgments. Within histori-
ography there is an analogue to this in the epoch, the
structure of the social milieu, the climate of thought or
action. The historical perspective of this type is ordinarily less explicit than its physical analogue, with
results not always fortunate for the discipline. Another
type of perspective in physics is an "external" one—
external to the actual subject matter but intrinsic to
the method—namely, the selection of central and or-
ganizational concepts in the process of systematizing,
or the selection of experimental techniques. The analogue of the "external" perspective in history is the
definition of the subject matter itself and the employ-
ment of appropriate categories in the treatment of
human affairs. But the differences between these disciplines in regard to perspective are not so great as
the differences which both have with a work of art. A
work of art does not reflect a perspective in the same
sense, and there is even one sense in which a work of
art "reflects" no perspective but only offers one. The
perspective of a physical or historical hypothesis is

adumbrated by the set of definitions and assumptions on the one hand, and the implications on the other, that constitute its expanded meaning. Not to be aware of these contextual directions is to misunderstand the judgment, that is, to make it genuinely doubtful whether we do or do not confound the given judgment with another. It is true that the social and biographical circumstances underlying, say, the composition of a novel correspond very roughly to the "defining conditions," and that the explorable values resident in it correspond to the "implications." But spectatorial invention in the response to art is much more possible and much more desirable. The latitude in determining what the "defining conditions" and the "implications" are is infinitely greater. And in very many instances we may choose to ignore these aspects with impunity. Our exploration of the work may be called incomplete but it cannot be called irrelevant or erroneous. Critical radicalism does not expose us to the danger of confounding the given judgment with another. If critical response is compelling, and if it is productive of reflexive query to the extent that the work of art is, it has already justified both itself and the work of art.

Now every judgment, active, assertive, or exhibitive, has potential ramifications so far as the articulation of it is concerned. In an assertive judgment, the indefinite class of implications constitutes the perspective by which it is articulatable. In certain exhibitive or active judgments (those which we agree to denominate single "acts" or single "works") the perspective is articulated

not by adding new judgments but by scrutinizing (manipulating and assimilating) the given judgment in reflexive or in inter-proceptive query. In the assertion we
trace the consequences; in the work of art or the moral
act we ascertain the responses. In both the assertion
and the work of art the perspective is, in part, the
amplification of the judgment. But in the assertion the
perspective is an amplification dictated by logical compulsion; in the work of art it is an amplification that
requires collaborative assent by the spectator. The
amplification of the assertion is the class of its consequences; the amplification of the work of art is the
class of its reflexive representations. Like the theory, the
work of art reflects something larger than itself; but
what it reflects is potential in a unique sense.

Philosophy, resembling both science and art, is both
assertive and exhibitive. But this statement requires
clarification. The distinction sometimes made between
critical and speculative philosophy, as complementaries,
does not help as much as it seems to at first blush. Speculative philosophy in the usual sense is not a body of
exhibitive judgments. And although it may be said that
speculative philosophy is exhibitive in its total character, it cannot be assumed that critical philosophy is
wholly assertive in character. For in the first place pro-
cedural analysis must always dwell largely on definitions in the sense of prescribed usages. Such definitions,
not being determinable as true or false in the usual
sense, are not assertions in the usual sense. Nor are they
exhibitive in a literal, exclusive sense. They are assertive to the extent that they serve as implicit standards

by which future assertions may be judged as lacking or adequate. They are exhibitive to the extent that, as prescriptions, they represent combinations of concepts and terms which appeal to a sense of satisfaction or to approval of the combination as a structure.

For the purpose of understanding how philosophy is both exhibitive and assertive a different type of distinction is required, between two phases of a philosophic perspective. In one of these, a philosophy constructs; in the other, it comments on the construction. On the one hand, it brings together a number of categories and develops them by analogy and metaphor and definition; in the other, it examines alternatives, excludes supposed implications, and justifies the categorial configurations in terms that do not make use of the categories. Construction and commentary—the commentary I have in mind is reflexive commentary, not polemic—are two modes of articulation, two ways in which a philosophic perspective comes into being. The constructive dimension of such a perspective constitutes its exhibitive character; the commentative, its assertive character. The mistake to avoid is the assumption that a philosophy has two parts, in one of which the judgments are exhibitive and in the other of which they are assertive. It is the perspective as a whole which must be regarded as a judgment-complex. A philosophy —and the same applies to a theory of science or a work of art—is not simply an aggregate of judgments but an order of interrelated judgments. The process of construction lays emphasis on "seeing" the meaning and on "feeling" the impact of the conceptual configuration.

Inevitably it is suggestive in character. It demands of the potential assimilator inferential and imaginative labor of a creative kind. The process of commentary lays emphasis on the "reference" of a philosophy, its applicability to the procept-complexes which men call "experience."

Ideally speaking, exhibitive and assertive judgment, building and vindicating in philosophy, enhance each other. The great practical difficulty in philosophic communication is how to distinguish between what is intended—or what should be regarded—as exhibitive and what as assertive. It is possible to reject a philosophic assertion while accepting a total perspective, and possible to reject a perspective while isolating and accepting an assertion. But more than that: it is possible to accept part of a perspective. For perspectives are not only sharable and adoptable but divisible. And this is fortunate for philosophy and for the growth of new perspectives.

Some philosophic perspectives will not easily lend themselves to commentative articulation, and all perspectives are refractory to some extent. This is simply one way of implying that exhibitive judgments cannot be translated into assertive judgments. Philosophic thinking conveys exhibitive judgment employing concepts and abstractions as its medium. The clearest recognition of the irreducibility of the exhibitive dimension in philosophy is to be found in the procedure of Plato's dialogues—the alternation between myth and dialectic. The appeal to myth has sometimes been construed as an escape from reason, from the intricate toils of analysis—a strange pronouncement on the author of *Theaetetus* and *Parmenides*. Or, somewhat more plausibly, the Platonic myth has been seen as a realization of the inadequacy of language to convey the entire message of reason, and as a consequent appeal to the evocative technique of art. This would be a satisfactory interpretation were it not for the fact that the myth is itself linguistic, an exploitation of an alternative linguistic medium; and were it not for the further fact that the myth is interwoven with dialectic, as in the *Republic*, where it is neither easy nor desirable to separate the overt and the covert myth, the myth as announced and the myth as intellectually embodied. The Platonic myth, the fictive tale, whether in its broader or narrower manifestations, is not an abandonment of judgment, for that is impossible. It is a recognition of the philosophic role of exhibitive judgment, and in this sense it is indeed an appeal to the technique of art.

A perspective might be interpreted as a kind of seeing if it were not the case that this makes it difficult to say without circularity that all seeing, perceptual and intellectual, takes place within a perspective. Seeing, after all, is not dissociable from living and from the movement of life. Hence perspective must be interpreted in terms of proception. A perspective is a kind of order, that kind of order in which a given set of natural complexes function as procepts for a given proceiver or (distributively) for a community of proceivers. To say that different proceivers share the same perspective is to say that the order in which each is related to a class of procepts is one and the same order. But some relations or orders are unique and unrepeated, even though they are, in part, of a common and repeatable character, and an instance of such an order would be the proceptive domain itself.

Perspective, then, is a property of proception, a natural and inevitable fact of a natural process. Assimilation and manipulation occur now in one perspective, now in another, and almost always within more than one. To the analogies of perspectival intersection, parallelism, and concentricity, we may add those of the perspectival spiral (which widens and alters) and the perspectival crossroads. But to emphasize the natural status of perspective—to emphasize, for instance, that "mystical insight" or "the light of reason" are cognitive preferences of the methodological animal—is to delimit its natural locus. We cannot regard everything whatever as a perspective. For Leibniz perspective is the primary fact of nature: nature is a class of perspectives. Aside from the misleading implication of his version, namely, that perspectives are unsharable and indivisible, it suggests the need of a distinction between a perspective and a system, between a more and a less general type of order. A system is a perspective considered solely in the light of its logical or existential properties. A system functions perspectivally, but it is possible to consider the properties of a system without reference to or regard for its ontological status in proception. Leibniz's substances are really systems. Now a system is divisible into sub-systems, and this indicates that it is necessary to distinguish further between the irreducibility and the indivisibility of a perspective. Since perspectives can intersect and be related concentrically, they are divisible (if we except the imminent proceptive domain) : there are narrower and broader perspectives. All perspectives may be called irreducible, however, in the sense that they are distinctive; and by definition, that which is distinctive or unique cannot be translated into another which is exactly equivalent, though of course it can be "translated" in the important sense of being rendered available. Perspectives are irreducible in the same sense that individuals are; indeed, it is in so far as they are individual that they are irreducible.

Whether perspective is a property that belongs to proception exclusively, or whether it is to be applied more broadly and regarded as a property of "organism" or even of any event, as Mead and Whitehead seem to suggest, is not an easy matter to decide. In the case of organisms of low degree, a perspective would have to mean simply a direction, or perhaps a direction that characterizes a vital interest. In the case of events, a perspective would have to mean simply the configuration of attributes that makes for uniqueness or individuality, even when propped by animistic or anthropomorphic categories. On so generalized a view of perspective it would be difficult to retain the properties of sharability and adoptability. "Perspective" would have to be identified with "situation." An event or an organism might be considered a situation of natural processes, and it might even be considered divisible into subsituations. But for events it would be nonsense to say, and for low-degree organisms it would be difficult to say, that they "adopt" or even that they "share" a situation. To say that two organisms share a situation would be only an inaccurate way of saying that they are both part of the situation, and to say that they adopt the situation would be a still more inept way of saying that they "enter" or become part of the situation. And they could hardly be said to "judge" alike in consequence of their common situation, unless "judgment" were equated with "behavior." If perspectives were nothing more than situations, the concept of communication would have to mean either (too narrowly) mutual stimulation, or (too broadly) mere relatedness. Philosophic generalization based on analogy needs to be compelling and not merely consistent; and this is why anthropomorphism courts difficulty.

Many philosophers have interpreted their discipline as one wherein perspectives of any kind are harmonized or, more usually, transcended. They have appealed to an Absolute exempt from the limitation of finitude and finite viewpoints. But other philosophers, as if despairing to transcend finitude altogether, have appealed to a kind of normative perspective, characterized by an alleged optimum of insight or of cognitive fertility. Instead of an ontological absolute they have posited an absolute intuition of one kind or another, a divine illumination, a light of nature. They have tried to surmount or to depreciate the natural circumstances of query, with its endless requirement of qualification. Fortunately, the perspectival value of their own philosophies is not annulled by the fact that their flight from perspective is a dream. Pathetically, their intuition is *their* intuition; the intuitive power they ascribe to all men is the power *they* interpret men to have; the very dream of flight is either a perspectival vision or a mad parade of symbols. They do not see that at best what all men presumably intuit could only be within a perspective common to all men. And if their deity or their absolute were viable, what could be clearer than that the perspective of such a being would always be measured by and distinguished from some finite perspective?

Another and older philosophic tradition affirmed the inevitability of perspective by declaring enigmatically that man is the measure of all things. Some of its exponents concluded that error is impossible because any judgment can be legitimated by the qualifying conditions of some perspective. And still other exponents found validation to be impossible because, among an indefinite number of possible perspectives, there could be no way of choosing one over all others. In effect, both the absolutistic and the Protagorean traditions deplore the evil of the point of view, the one concluding that the evil necessarily entails an opposing good, the other, that the evil is the best of all possible goods. For perhaps a century now a philosophic minority has begun to be less dismayed by the natural ultimacy of finitude, and has begun to discern the role of perspective as a natural condition of judgment. It is at least a possibility that this attitude has been fortified by recent developments in the sciences. Yet a tendency is widespread, on the part of both philosophers and laymen, to think and speak as if perspective represented a special manifestation of knowing rather than as if knowing were an illustration of perspective. We speak,

for instance, of either being "immersed in events" or
of "seeing events in perspective." We speak of the advantage which "historical perspective" confers, as if
perspective implied seeing from afar and as if it were
not the very condition of seeing at all. Or we often
speak of perspective as a property of sense-perception,
and as such we employ it as instrumental in the theory
of space, without wishing to generalize it. The optical
usage is perhaps the most common literal one. Not to
generalize is unphilosophical; to extend the analogy to
an extreme length is to risk extravagance. I have been
suggesting in this chapter that when perspective is associated with judgment, in the generalized sense of the
latter term that we have been employing, a satisfactory
mean has been reached. To make perspective an attribute of all things is to lose sight of the original factor
of "seeing." To make it, on the other hand, an indisso-
ciable factor of judgment not only does justice to the
suggestion of seeing but helps to clarify an important
consideration, that, visually or proceptively, seeing is
actualized by judging.

Every judgment, we said, occurs within a perspective or, if we prefer, expresses a perspective. But just
what is it that is expressed? How do we determine the
components of a perspective? Where does it begin and
where does it end? What leads us to identify a judgment as part of one perspective rather than of another?
These questions are not insuperable. The first thing to
realize is that to speak of a beginning or end, or of
precise boundaries, is misleading. The precise perspectives are the artificial ones like a formal calculus. But

these are few and far indeed among the perspectives of man. I have spoken of some perspectives as opaque. But to be opaque does not mean to be well-ordered. A perspective may be narrow and even exclusive, yet very imprecise in character. The orthodox religions fall into this class. Every orthodoxy tries to build a wall around itself; but no one is clear, and certainly not the orthodox, where the wall begins or ends. Barriers are not necessarily boundaries. Predicates like "beginning" and "end" apply only with awkwardness to a proceptive order. A proceptive order is not a container. The proceptive domain is the perspective of greatest comprehensiveness for the individual, whereby all his other perspectives define themselves. "Whereby" does not mean to imply that all of a man's perspectives must be reflexively referred by him to his own life, or that his own life is necessarily part of the data and content of these perspectives.

Now we suggested in Chapter I that an individual could be regarded as being part of an indefinite number of situations, and that each such situation represented a variation of the floating proceptive domain. A perspective is the order by which a given situation may be defined. The floating domain is the class of situations in which a proceiver is represented. But it was also suggested that what a "situation" was, is determinable in the last analysis by convention, and the same is true of a perspective. It is important to emphasize "in the last analysis." The factors making for coherency arise primarily within the living situation and only secondarily by viewing the situation critically. A moral problem brings with it a host of conditions which enable us at least roughly to regard certain alternatives as relevant and others as irrelevant to its resolution. A moral situation is a grouping of circumstances and attitudes that are relevant to one another. What factors are or are not relevant, what factors do or do not belong together cannot be decided in advance of a situation or point of view. A chain of compulsions is usually at the core of every situation; it forms the nucleus on the basis of which we abstractly characterize the nature of the situation and on the basis of which we (conventionally) decide its limits. To say that it is difficult to determine what is and what is not relevant to a given situation is really to say that a number of situations are intermingled; and similarly, to say that it is difficult to determine what is and is not part of a given perspective is to admit that a single perspective which we are trying to bound is not yet discriminated from its intersecting perspectives.

How can a theory of philosophies as perspectives account for the historical fact that these perspectives have been criticized and have apparently remained subject to criticism? Does a perspectival interpretation of the philosophic enterprise eliminate the meaning and value of polemic? The question is part of a larger question, What makes any criticism at all possible and effective? I shall grapple with this larger question in the next chapter. But one consideration of fundamental importance enables us to answer the narrower question first. When we speak of philosophic perspectives we are not speaking of insular private idioms. Philosophies are not personal feelings or unique personal attributes. The optical analogy should not be abused: it is not the sense of vision alone that individuals possess but the objects and relations that are common to other visual perspectives. Nor should the linguistic analogy be abused: individuals who speak different cultural languages can find behavioral community in the basic gestures and patterns that make the languages themselves possible. Now community of philosophic understanding has been and is potentially at least as great as community of sight and community of speech. Philosophic perspectives, even where they fail to overlap and intersect, attempt to achieve universality. In philosophy the individuality of an idiom is likely to be greater than that of the subject matter it manipulates. The philosopher, then, in formulating his categories and principles, represents a world that is always to some extent available to other perspectives. But inevitably he goes further than this. In shaping his structure he presumes to represent other perspectives than his own. He is not simply reporting his impressions but making a tacit recommendation that his results fit other perspectives and that in some sense they are juster to these perspectives than the formulation which others design for them. In the very framing of his philosophic structure, therefore, the philosopher already incorporates a principle of criticism. He cannot make reference only to his proceptive direction, to his "experience." On the contrary, it is a potential trait of all judgment, and of philosophic judgment in particular, to transcend the proceptive circumstances that breed it and to offer itself for common assimilation.

The principle of criticism is explicitly present in the commentative dimension of philosophy. The philosopher who justifies himself discursively cannot preclude potential justification offered by others. Nor can he, by the same token, preclude potential correction by others if he is open to correction and amplification by himself. The commentative dimension of philosophy distinguishes it from art: and this is one other way of saying that philosophy is assertive as well as exhibitive. It is, so to speak, art which is discursively self-conscious. But here again, we must not commit oversimplification by supposing that only a fixed part of every philosophy is subject to criticism. It is the perspective as an exhibitive whole that is affected by criticism. Since perspectives are sharable and adoptable, and since they overlap, philosophers can presume to speak for one another, given the imaginative essentials required. Not only is it theoretically conceivable that a philosopher can augment the articulation of another's perspective; this is actually done when one philosopher systematizes or synthesizes another's insights, reinterprets his language, or draws implications from his principles. Such contributions are constructive and not simply commentative articulations; but of course they may take the form of constructive changes rather than amplifications. When criticism is on the commentative plane it may likewise be ampliative or nugatory. Hostile criticism does not necessarily imply the insistence by one philosopher that another think the way he himself does or that he abandon his conceptual preferences. This would be grotesque as well as arrogant. Negative criticism can only mean that an alleged justification is not established by the conceptual materials deployed. That criticism in this sense should be efficacious follows simply from the fallibility of man. It is no more surprising that a philosopher should be unable to sustain the promise of his own insights or be faithful to them than that he should be able to do so.

A philosophic perspective invades the perspectives of all other philosophies when it lays claim to consistency, as it implicitly must if it is to have philosophic rather than exclusively poetic or biographical significance. Much of the criticism in the history of philosophy has been directed to formal inconsistency or to internal incongruity of one or another kind. If philosophers, through inconsistency, can violate the common rules on which the very being of assertive utterance depends, they can equally well violate the traits interpretable in all perspectives, either by feeble delineation or by impoverished categories. The minimal requirement of achievement in a philosophy is that it compel imaginative assent and arouse the sense of encompassment even where it fails of cognitive acceptance. This presupposes a high ideal, but only in the light of such an ideal can philosophic criticism function. We can demand of philosophy, if not of art, that it be better than it is, however good it may be. We can demand of a perspective, not that it translate itself into our own perspective, but that it be significant enough for us to desire the translation and to approximate it in reflexive query.

Meaning—I stress as central the participial character

of the term—is the process by which a perspective is shaped or revealed, that is, articulated in communication. The perspective may be an individual human situation or an abstract formal system. Now a definition of this type can adequately account for active and exhibitive judgment. Thus, in the case of music we could not accept an identification of "meaning" with "reference," for we do not ordinarily assume a referent. Similarly, the conception of meaning as consisting in a "method of verification" does not apply without great ambiguity to active judgments. A general theory of the foundations of utterance must do justice to the broad conception of meaning expressed, for instance, by the usage "What is the meaning of this act?" Some philosophers have spoken of meaning as "intent." But this term, felicitous at first blush in its application to active judgment, is precarious in its suggestions. It is true that meaning, as James saw in the deeper phases of his analysis, is "meaning for us"; it is, as we have preferred to put it, a property of the communicative enterprise of men, and it is not an "objective essence" which men glimpse from a distance. But the notion of intent must not overlook the fact that when we "mean" we express and reflect a commitment, and not simply either an intention or an impulse. The commitment is the perspective within which we are functioning or which a product mirrors.

I said that meaning is the process by which a perspective is *shaped* or revealed. A musical work, a novel, a building constitutes a judgment which is itself best seen as a perspective. A meaning comes into being when the exhibitive judgment is framed—materials are "given" a meaning. The meaning of the judgment is "found" or "discovered" in the reshaping of the judgment (the discovery of the perspective) accomplished by the process of assimilative query. The "meaning" of the exhibitive judgment is determined and molded in the (indefinite) scrutiny by which it is critically reanimated. (Nothing is more dubious—nor indeed more difficult to make sense of—than the view that "aesthetic response" is of an "immediate" character.) The perspective explored is the product itself, with its fluid boundaries, though it always is possible, and may often be desirable, also to scrutinize it within a perspective larger than itself. The elasticity or variety which may belong to the meaning of certain judgments is made possible by the fact that any judgment, in being assimilated, is contained in or intersects with the perspective of the assimilator. The product is not annulled, it is interpreted: all judgments are. And it is always the product that "has" the meaning, however contextualized—that reflects a perspective subject to articulation.

The degree of variability in meaning that a judgment will have cannot, however, be determined from the mere fact that it is exhibitive or active or assertive. The purposes for which we frame assertive judgments usually make it imperative that we cultivate agreement rather than difference. Such goals as explanation, generalization, or inference are imperiled by variability in meaning. But the ideals of assertive judgment are not to be confused with the contingent circumstances within which it is as often subject to variability of interpre-

tation as active or exhibitive judgment. In the two latter modes of judgment variability of interpretation can
actually augment the articulation of the perspective.
But variability here too has its limits. We do and must
distinguish competent from incompetent criticism and
elucidation, even though we cannot set up antecedent
rules for good interpretation.

Meaning, then—and here we may allow the substan-
tival or adjectival usage—is a property of products
within a communicative situation, social or reflexive.
And variability of meaning depends upon the variability of communicative situations and needs. The tendency of many philosophers to ascribe meaning to assertion only, or to dignify such meaning as alone of "cognitive" value, springs from the same considerations that
limit "judgment" to assertive judgment, as well as from
an inadequate theory of communication. To clarify a
meaning is to identify some perspective within social or
reflexive communication and to delineate a relationship either of the product with other products or within
the product itself. For obscurity, ambiguity, or misunderstanding to arise means that we have lost sight of the
perspective to which a communicative situation commits us.

To interpret meaning in these terms is not to add a
theory which aims to abolish other theories so much as
to determine a set of properties of a general and comprehensive character. Thus I do not intend to say that
"meaning" can never be equated with "reference" or
with "defining formula" or with "habit of behavior" (a
special kind of defining formula) or with "psychological

effects." I mean rather (1) that articulation of a perspective is the factor present in all cases where one or another of these equivalents is held to be present. In this sense a view which is thus more general is at the same time more precise, and would not confound a generic characteristic of meaning with one of its species. And I mean also to indicate (2) that in the light of the generic characteristic the more special criteria ought to be reexamined and perhaps in some instances more broadly defined.

Consider, for example, the view that the meaning of a judgment is its "reference." We agreed that for active and exhibitive judgments there may be no reference in the usual denotative sense. But even where we may wish to speak in such terms, we should have to broaden them by a satisfactory reinterpretation. Thus in so far as a philosophic theory has a reference, it may be to a type of complex data not readily identifiable in perception or in measurement. The denotation of a philosophic concept may have no customary name, and it may require a particular kind of imaginative charity. For instance, when my philosophic subject matter is the proceptive direction, my means of identification must be mediated by numerous other concepts. I am making reference to man, but not just to man; to the individual, but not exclusively. We are more likely to be impatient with philosophic denotation if we labor under the illusion that there is such a thing as "pure" or "perfect" reference. Any reference at all is mediated by concepts and assumptions. If a sign were entirely demonstrative it would be entirely inarticulate and hence would be no sign. Hegel and Peirce and Royce combine to teach that without interpretation there is no denotation and therefore no communication. Philosophic language and philosophic meaning only make greater demands on the inventiveness with which we pursue the process of validation. They demand of the assimilator the resources to hold together in conceptual imagination what may not be found together in perception. The universality to which they appeal is to be found in proceptive parallelism and in the communities to which all men belong.

VI
VALIDATION

As events in nature the products of men are complete and inexpugnable. But as potential vehicles of communication they stand in need of a certain kind of actualization which, we shall suggest, can never be wholly achieved: they require to be validated. In the last analysis validation is justification. The idea of justification, to be sure, will by itself hardly illuminate the idea of validation. And to some, it will even seem to becloud the problem. Is it not "correct" or "warranted" justification by which judgments are consummated? But a moment's reflection indicates the vacuity of the qualification. To call a judgment "correct" or "warranted" is the same as calling it "valid," and validation could hardly be regarded as valid justification. The term "justification" has always suffered from an ambiguity. In the two usages "What he did was justified" and "He justified himself by claiming illness" the former seems to imply an impersonal verdict of fate, the latter an unstable and more or less arbitrary apologetic. The discrepancy vanishes on the expansion of an ellipsis. Strictly, the second statement, when taken in the more literal sense of the first, means to convey "He *attempted* to justify himself" (by means of a claim). In this more literal sense, to justify an act or a statement is the same thing as for that act or statement to be justified or validated. We need, then, to extend the analysis far beyond the synonymity of the terms.

Validation is a process of appraisal. The customary forms of validation, like the verification of a theory or the trial of a lawsuit, are systematized or conventionalized forms of appraisal. Every judgment, we intimated earlier, is a tacit appraisal. That is to say, it can be expanded to reveal as part of its meaning some discrimination, selection, or decision; it is an extraction from an environment of something specific to the exclusion of something else. Validation is sometimes conceived of as an activity performing a definite type of proceptive function, for instance, the elimination of doubt (Peirce), the resolution of a problem (Dewey), the mitigation of blocked conduct (Mead). These conceptions are remarkable in their depth and in their applicability. Yet they are not general enough. They confuse validation with inquiry and inquiry with query. And they err in regarding validation as the erasure of a specific disharmony, a function which may or may not belong more properly to inquiry. Validation comprehends more than even query, for it is predicable of the career of products which may not be designed to further reflexive communication. Every judgment implicitly seeks justification, because of the commitment incurred by the proceiver in judging. The primordial claim latent in human existence itself is the claim of valid continuance. Inventiveness implies satisfaction of a methodic intent or demand, a demand which as such does not necessarily imply disharmony. Yet this demand is the very core of the validation process. Validation aims to secure, not necessarily to resolve. The resolution of problems is one form of achieving security. By security I do not mean acquired complacency. The spirit of inquiry is an instance and not the antithesis of what I mean: it is a technique of detecting insecurity in ideas in order to attain greater security. The process of validation is no disguise for the worship of quiescence. The intellectually corrupt are always forced to seek validation in spite of themselves, because of their overarching proceptive commitment. In a process which is inevitable, the extent to which they succeed is an entirely separate question. Even when, as in science, art, or philosophy, we are systematically dedicated to the abandonment or alteration of the products we have held, it is for the purpose of preserving the better. Those who, like the religious dogmatists, are concerned exclusively to affirm principles at the expense of query, are the most insecure of men. The history of religion is a history of recrudescent demonstrations and reaffirmations, and these have flourished most when, as in the Middle Ages, the professed enemies of the defended faith have been fewest.

The formalized processes of scientific explanation are devices by which the proceptive quest for security is clarified and guided. The extent to which irrelevant species of security are isolated from inquiry is one of the measures of rigor in science. Validation is always an enterprise of preservation; it is sometimes a search for perfection. In principle, the great disciplines of human query are disciplines of validation in both respects.

What I am suggesting is that validation is not necessarily associated with method. Methodical, purposeful
validation—validation become critical and self-conscious—is part of formal search, that is, structural-
ized query. But certain characteristics of methodical
validation may be found also in proceptive or omnipresent validation. In both there is a utilization of some
source of judgment such as past experience. For methodical validation, past experience is the fund of past
instances, the ground of generalization. For proceptive
validation, past experience is the basis of familiarity
with the present circumstances of judging. Similarly, in
both methodical and proceptive validation there is a
certain pattern or mode by which the source of judgment is brought to bear on present judgment: in both,
spontaneous insight is the unregulated use of the available fund of objects and products.

In the proceptive process, validation is no less fundamental than discovery. Judgments reflect discovery and
propose validation or the preservation of their content,
though validation as such does not necessarily imply
that what we seek to preserve we never wish to discard.
To recognize discovery as proceptively original but to
deny the same status to validation would be to exag-
gerate the assimilative dimension of life and under-
estimate the manipulative. To regard validation as a
special enterprise helps indirectly to nourish the error
that cognitive value belongs either exclusively or primarily to assertive judgment. The concept of validation
is confused by the fact that the issue of what does and
what does not have cognitive value has never been

made very clear. Ordinarily, for instance, we ask whether "immediate experience" or "intuition" can be regarded as cognitive in nature. But the answer of yes or no depends on a distinction between cognitive decision and cognitive accumulation. Both intuitionists and fallibilists usually think in terms of the former—in terms of whether a sensation or an axiom does or does not render a cognitive verdict. But a sensation or a general principle may be cognitively indecisive and yet cognitively relevant; it may have small cognitive value in isolation but may contribute greatly in an ultimate proceptive reckoning, or even in the upshot of formal inquiry. In the same way, the usual question about the cognitive value of exhibitive judgments like works of art sees these judgments in formal terms and tacitly applies to them the type of cognitive standard that is universally recognized to apply to assertions. Once we see them as cognitively cumulative—as indeed we had best interpret all assertions as well—we can recognize their candidacy for validation. I have earlier suggested, in more general terms, that by definition no procept can be cognitively irrelevant, though quantitatively speaking most procepts are cognitively negligible.

All validation is a process of guessing and applying—good and bad guessing, good and bad applying. If the notion suggests itself that all living is largely a matter of guessing and applying, this restates pretty well the foregoing conception of validation as a proceptive category. Peirce held that all explanatory invention is basically a process of guessing; and the notion may be generalized to characterize the entire web of inductive science. A theoretical network is a complex guess rendered strong by the independent success of simpler or subordinate guesses. This means that the durability of the entire fabric is greater than that of its components. The same is true of any human structure. The cultural traits of a society are stabler than its political forms; political traditions are stabler than party platforms; the gross proceptive domain is stabler than the floating proceptive domain. The idea of science as a conjectural structure preempting the future with progressive success is remote from the classical or rationalistic conception of science as an elaboration of axioms. In the practice of inductive science the criterion for basic principles is pervasiveness of application rather than breadth of intuitive insight. The classical conception still dominates a great part of contemporary metaphysics and a still greater part of contemporary theology.

In what we call moral conduct it is perhaps not difficult to see that guessing and applying are fundamental. The choice between alternatives, which moralists have thought to illustrate sentiment, intelligence, or moral sense, may illustrate all or none of these, but it is a guess as long as prophecy and omniscience do not belong to the chooser. The guiding moral tone determines the application of moral patterns to specific situations. The more morally self-conscious the chooser, the greater his analytical power (though not necessarily his physical power) in the application of his moral past. But that guessing and applying are fundamental to the process of artistic creation may seem more debatable.

What the artist applies is what everyone else applies, the fund of his impressions and information, or more accurately, the effect which nature and culture have had in the form of his most fundamental perspective, the gross domain. What he guesses about is his own intent. If this appears to be contingent for its truth upon a special kind of personality, it is probably because the term "guessing" ordinarily implies a haphazard process. But guessing is presuming or anticipating, and guesses do not arise *in vacuo*. Scientific hypotheses have as their natural basis not only a puzzling situation but the potential directions of judgment which belong to any puzzling situation. Artistic guesses require for their validation manipulation of a medium, whether the manipulation be direct or envisioned. Guessing is a way of articulating. One can articulate or clarify oneself by simply discarding those judgments which happen to impede the actual process of communication. One then, in a sense, makes one's pronouncements more luminous. But the dark judgments remain dark and the light light, and the latter are merely dissociated from the former. To articulate in this way is often the function of the propagandist or popular journalist; it cannot be the function of the artist, scientist, or philosopher. In this sense it would be false or at least questionable to say that the more articulate judgments are also the most valid. Easy delivery is not so good as purposive groping. Validation is a way of justifying, not merely a way of dismissing, judgments. It seems clear that when traditional idealism emphasized the identity of "meaning" and "truth," the "meaning" involved

could not have been the result of articulation in this illusory sense. It must rather have come from the kind
which brings a judgment to the point of possible ratification through the dissipation of proceptive or communal dissent. Artistic guessing means discriminating
among a number of insights which are collectively but
not individually compulsive. The artist validates a given
insight by manipulating his medium in accordance with
it until his manipulation is consummated by decision.
To the notion of artistic validation I shall return presently.

A judgment has an essential past and an essential
future. "Essential" because its past and future involve
more than mere coming to be and enduring. A judgment is rendered possible by previous judgments and is
bound to previous judgments by the relations either of
suggestion or presupposition. It may be suggested
(hypothetically) or necessarily implied by other judgments. The suggestion of one assertive judgment by
others is expressible as an inferential form: it is the way
in which hypotheses (or new judgments) arise.[11] The
proceptive domain hosts a miscellany of suggestions,
presuppositions, and obligations to validate. When we
validate we are concerned not merely with a given judgment but with the body of prior judgments connected
with it. This notion is well attested, so far as the philosophy of inductive science is concerned, by the research
of about a century now. But I use the term "connected" because it is general enough to comprehend the
interrelations of active and of exhibitive judgments as
well as of assertive: one judgment may be said to be

"connected" with another if, in some perspective, it is required for the articulation of that judgment, or if that judgment is required for its articulation. Which of the judgments is to be regarded as "prior" or "more fundamental" depends on the direction from which we approach the perspective, or the direction in which the perspective is being articulated. Because of the communal structure of scientific inquiry, there is less latitude than in other modes of query so far as the direction of inference is concerned. The commitments of a theory in science are far greater with respect to established judgment than in art or even philosophy.

Like the judgment, the validation-situation as such also comprehends a past. The past comprehended may be a methodological or an ontological past, or both. There is always a methodological past, which is simply the validation-process itself prior to any designated moment of it. Every process of query is a methodological (as well as a proceptive or communal) history. Artistic invention, experimentation in positive science, or demonstration are at least temporal processes, whatever else they are. Validation in positive science, however, entails an ontological past in a sense in which mathematical demonstration as such does not. In pure mathematics, as in natural science, the validation of the conclusion comes last: the theorem, like the theory, is a result and a relative termination. But in natural science the validation would not be what it is, did not the world have the traits of actuality it has. Past inquiry is knowledge of occurrence in nature up to the present. Any hypothesis presupposes natural sequences or traits already defined, and sequences or traits which it is itself defining. It cannot suppose that it is inventing traits but only that it is interpreting what is typical of nature's history and habits. In artistic query the ontological past plays a somewhat different role. What the world is and has been is the vehicle and the occasion of reshaping rather than of foreseeing and formulating. The artist is inexorably faced by the world, limited by his medium, and concerned with appropriating the world's engrossing complexes instead of predicting its structure.

A judgment stands to future judgments as past judgments stand to it. Assertive judgments have an indefinite number of implications; active and exhibitive judgments have indefinite potentialities for further invention, action, and assimilation. From consideration of the bidimensional connection of each judgment, it should be clear why no judgment can validate itself. Assertive judgments cannot establish their own truth, active and exhibitive judgments cannot establish themselves as irrevocably approvable, either at a given time or for all time. Of any judgment and its claim, it is always possible to ask, simply but irresistibly, why? It is monstrous to suppose that every fact discernible about a product, and every suggestion or implication latent in it, is already possessed; yet all such facts are pertinent to the being of the product and to its validation. To say that a judgment is "self-validating" is an elliptical way of saying that it needs no validation, and this in turn means, inconsistently enough, that we can discern validity while ignoring the components and conditions by which its discernment is made possible.

Any instance of validating leads to a consummation. Whatever this may amount to for the gods, for men it consists in some kind of approval or ratification. We declare a judgment valid when we see in it a relative finality, and when we assent to it as requiring no further manipulation. Our assent is ordinarily compounded of conventional and compulsive elements, but in either case the important consideration is that we deem the accepted judgment (or judgment-complex) sufficient so far as its own alterability is concerned. With respect to their validation, exhibitive judgments differ from assertive in at least one significant respect: their compulsive elements are not evidential in character. In all modes of judgment there can be instances of private validation. As many philosophers are repelled by the idea that validation can be private as by the idea that validation must be public. If the assumption that validation is a process of appraisal be accepted, it is clear why validation can be a private process. Some perspectives, involving unique and possibly unrepeatable situations, may carry with them unique appraisals relative to individuals. This is very likely the case in all of artistic invention. Transition from one formative step to another may be compulsive, but in the process of invention it can nevertheless constitute a validation of one step. An artist may revise his earlier judgment: aesthetic alteration is no less possible than scientific; but validation, after all, depends upon conditions. The "conditions" in science means the evidence at hand; in art, it means the field of choice available for insight and calculation. When assertive judgments are privately validated, it is not because the circumstances are *unique;* it is because they are *restricted.* When I judge the character of a momentary feeling, I alone am in a position to confirm the assertion, to appraise its adequacy. But the mode of confirmation can always be reproduced; the situation can be reenacted so far as the validation is concerned.

The validation of active judgments is their moral justification; although to change the form of this statement and declare that moral conduct can be validated may sound more intelligible. Active judgments resemble assertive and differ from exhibitive in that one judgment may compel another evidentially; they differ from assertive and resemble exhibitive in that sometimes their validation may be not only private but unique. One act may justify another—it may make the other the sole alternative according to a given standard or end, that is, in a given perspective. It may be the evidence for the rightness of another. And it may be private in the sense that the prior standard to which the evidence is related may be that of a single individual; or in the sense that only to a single individual's perspective may a given act be vouchsafed as evidence. No active (or any other) judgments which are private, are private in the sense that they are indescribable or uninvestigable. But it is perfectly conceivable that only for one person, among many who understand a description, might a validating circumstance be morally compulsive.

Ordinarily when philosophers speak of "ethical judgments" they mean verbal expressions relating to conduct. On the present view, of course, moral acts are judgments no less than verbal moral expressions. I suggested earlier that acts can also function as assertive or as exhibitive judgments. Many philosophers believe that verbal moral expressions, though assertive, are a very different kind of assertion from "factual judgments"; and many others believe that they are not assertions at all, and hence, in their usage, not judgments at all. Interestingly enough, many of these philosophers would agree that conduct can be "appraised," but would deny that verbal moral expressions can be "validated." But to validate an act is to determine its justifiability (in terms of specified ends) under certain conditions; and to appraise it as right or wrong is precisely to take a position with respect to its validation. Traditionally, then, one reason for not thinking in terms of validating acts is that appraisal is considered to be generically different from validation. But perhaps the chief reason why we so seldom think in terms of validating acts is that acts are held to be intrinsically different from "propositions." Propositions, it is said, are or can be regarded as, literally, proposals, whereas acts are accomplishments. The former can be tested and established because they can be replaced and disposed of, whereas acts are ineradicable. Or, propositions are regarded as the formulation of acts (or facts), which constitute their subject matter. You can validate a formulation but not its subject matter. Propositions can be "entertained"; facts are "there," accepted.

Certain presuppositions hidden in these views cannot withstand analysis. First, that "proposition" and "fact" are entirely distinct categories. Certainly no one would want to lump the two together and deny any rationale to the use of the respective terms. The important consideration is: In virtue of which properties do we want to make a distinction, and in virtue of which other properties do we want to make an identification? In so far as "propositions" and "facts" relate to the life of a man, they are procepts. In so far as we wish to distinguish between logical and ontological relations in a very broad sense, the usage is no doubt justified. But by the same token, in so far as we wish to determine the generic traits of proception and communication, certain common characteristics make the distinction between assertive and active judgment much more fundamental than that between "proposition" and "fact" (or "act"). The proverb that actions can speak louder than words simply happens to be metaphysically correct.

Second, the presupposition that propositions and facts alike are discrete entities. But every proposition presupposes and implies other propositions, and every fact is inseparable from facts that have occurred before it and other facts for which it is a basis. The discrete proposition and the discrete fact are at best useful abstractions which are always to some degree conventional. Third, that language and the world, discourse and existence, symbol and symbolized are compulsive and absolute distinctions. But language is certainly one mode of "existence," symbols are one manifestation of nature and things natural; and theoretically, any fact, object, or situation can serve as a sign or symbol capable of representing some other fact, object, or situation. The breakdown of this classical distinction has been adumbrated by a relatively small number of philosophers with superior insight in the analysis of meaning. The concept of judgment that is here employed is designed as one way of categorizing such an insight. The species of human utterance are not limited to the *kinds* of human *symbols* (symbol and act falsely taken as a fixed distinction) but are broadened to include different modes of judgment, which collectively define the productivity of the human process. Any effecting by man, then, constitutes an utterance or judgment, and every utterance is subject to validation, even if it be not actually validated.

Though the predicate "valid" can be applied to any judgment, it cannot be applied in all circumstances. There are definite conditions under which it makes sense to call a judgment valid. For example, the use of the term for an exhibitive judgment derives its sense from the circumstances and intent that belong to the process of shaping. It makes sense for the shaper of a marble product to validate it as his evolved judgment. But ordinarily—that is, without qualification—it makes very little sense for another to echo the application of the predicate and declare the same judgment indeed valid. Critical analysis in terms of validity, the procedure whereby the critic brings an aesthetic standard to bear on the exhibitive judgment, for the most part sounds ridiculous. The reason is that the alternatives to the judgment, and the life of its sequential relation to other judgments, are lost after its production. For the artist the perspective that generates a particular judgment is an induplicable order. In the case of assertive and even of most active judgments the situation is different. For these are not induplicable in the same sense. In the most commonplace of exhibitive judgments— the whittling of a piece of wood, the arrangement of dress—a certain residual gap is established between one proceiver (or community) as primarily the manipulator and another as primarily the assimilator. The sharability of the perspective of the creator is established by conventional disregard of something essential in its development. An assertive judgment, on the other hand, permits continual reenactment of the validating conditions. The unique traits in its utterance are inessential and the circumstances of its origin and growth are irrelevant so far as its meaning and validity are concerned.

A work of art, then, may be said most properly to be validated by its maker (or makers) in the process of its contrivance and enunciation. This process of (exhibitive) validation occurs in the kind of perspective that is assimilable but not duplicable. It consists in the completion or implementation of one part of a product by another. The parts of a product may be said to ratify or consummate one another. A musical phrase, indifferent or even banal in itself, is validated by its musical allocation; a movement of the body is validated by the context which makes it part of a dance; stones carried about are insignificant except when the activity is justified by their organization in a wall. And in general, human contrivance, artistic practice, validates its exhibitive judgments by determining and redetermining their place in more complex products. This conception embraces collaborative as well as strictly "individual" invention. What is important is the uniqueness of exhibitive query and the exhibitive perspective, not the singleness of a man. In this sense the critic of a work of art can, collaboratively, contribute to the validation because he can contribute to the completion. And he can contribute to the completion by extending the perspectival order and discovering new properties in it. "Completion" is a process with degrees, and in its present signification it suggests a relatively final validation effected conventionally by an assent of the contriver. From the latter's standpoint the purview of the validation may vary greatly: for instance, the stone wall may itself not be deemed justified apart from its relation to a group of other structures and a landscape. Society usually demands units of work, and so for the most part do the professional artists of history. *A* poem, *a* building are the understandable vehicles by which attention is focused and query simplified. Easily isolable products make critical appraisal easier: the impulse to adjudicate is of course fundamental to man, for better or worse. It would be good if sometimes we could assimilate the products of exhibitive query with a creative indecision. The product would have a prospective and retrospective dimension with respect to other products and to the rest of the world, yet it would be valued for being the part of the world that it is.

But if we would not object to the relative unfamiliarity of the designation, there is for exhibitive judgments a second kind of validation that can be said to be posterior to the process of contrivance. It is the kind of validation that does not imitate assertive query by seeking the alternatives of acceptance or rejection but that rather presupposes degrees of assimilability. The stronger the product, the greater the opportunity for qualitative assimilation. The greater the impact of an exhibitive judgment on the critical sensibility of its social audience, the greater the degree of its validation. Such an impact should not be confused with "social approval." The validity of a work of art lies in the extent to which it modifies human query; its longevity and repute are significant only in so far as they mirror the depth of the modification. This kind of validation belongs to common and standardized as well as to unique products. Whether the product be a familiar machine or a type of dinnerware, its inherent validation in the form of social use is measurable by the character of its permanency. Assimilation of any kind can be deep or shallow, more or less sustained, better or poorer in its articulateness. Not all judgments need to be actually pronounced valid in order to justify themselves. Each successive enterprise of articulation critically aroused by a work of art is a step in its validation. To deny that a product's vitality, its status as an object of interest, or its endorsement is a kind of validity is to blur the relations among the modes of human appraisal and to be blind to the generic community of these modes. It is primarily for the artist to legislate the relation of the parts of the product to one another; when we legislate otherwise, we create anew and establish one more induplicable order. But in our critical query we help to determine the very character of the product in human assimilation and hence its relative value in human affairs.

In the process of validation, a judgment is rendered secure within a given perspective. It is perhaps mathematically conceivable that some judgment should be valid for all possible perspectives; but in any particular instance such a supposition is stultifying and presumptuous. A judgment may be said to be valid in a given perspective if there is no reason, desire, or need to alter it. This definition is imprecise, but at present I do not know how to better it without sacrificing its generality. Does it follow from this view that virtually any human product is "valid"? The Greek philosophers were profoundly disturbed by the implication: it seemed to eliminate the possibility of incompetence, error, or malfeasance. It seemed to threaten a shallow relativism whereby anybody could be as right as anybody else, since what was to him, was, to at least a limited extent. The same fears beset a good many philosophers today, who distrust and usually misunderstand the concept of perspective. The fear that this concept conflicts with the facts of communication is of a similar character. It is a simple fact, an indubitable datum, that men communicate; but it is likewise a simple fact, as we have seen, that men share perspectives. And it is a simple fact that men err, but the correlative fact to be associated with the notion of perspective is that men can be and usually are ignorant of the properties of their own perspectives. The most, then, that can be said—although it is extremely important, and far different from the view that no one can judge erroneously —is that for *any* judgment *some* validating perspective can be determined or defined. Let us elaborate on these ideas.

My version of what occurs within my proceptive domain—what happens or appears or develops in relation to me—is incontestable, if I can report correctly what that is, to myself or to another, and if, further, I fully understand the limits of my perspective and judge in accordance with it. The "if" here is a very large one. It is notoriously difficult to separate out the testimony of our senses from the opinions received by us and the habits inculcated in us, the results of our imagination and reasoning from the subtle indoctrination of the many communities in which we stand. We hold opinions and affirm convictions which, strictly, are neither opinions nor convictions, but formulae. Many of our judgments are responses and not products of reflexive query or even faithful mirrors of our "experience." Perhaps it may be safely said that for the most part we are uncertain (though we do not consider ourselves uncertain) of what we desire and what we sense and what we think. In part this is a consequence of the instability of man; in part, also, it is the result of the visible and invisible commitments of the individual. Articulation is an imperative of life and of expression. For the process of articulation determines ultimately what we want and see and believe. Judgment, of any kind, does not spring full-blown from the proceptive direction and present itself for articulation; articulation is part of the being and destiny of judgment.

The individual, then, is not "entitled" to whatever he utters. He must substantiate; he must validate or render secure the products that emanate from his own perspectives. He must define and discover his proceptive commitments and accept as data of validation the critical query of others who may share some part of the same perspective. The reason why, for instance, the individual cannot wholly prescribe his own morality is that the moral perspectives within which he thinks and acts cannot be his alone; his active judgments cannot all relate to him as their sole subject; and his desires and preferences remain to be articulated by a process of communication that transcends his own visible intent. Similarly, he cannot hold that whatever "science" asserts "his" science excludes or negates. He cannot have a science of his own however much he wants one. He is subject to evidential compulsion even when he is unaware of it; his conclusions are not likely to be self-consistent if they are inconsistent with universal testimony; and he cannot by an act of will command a large world for small vision, a ramified gross domain for isolated momentary desire. What is true of individual perspective is no less true of communal perspective. A revealed religion cannot claim that what is true and false for science is, respectively, false and true for its "religious perspective." The process of validating assertive judgments about the complexes of nature entails certain commitments which are simply not properties of such a perspective. For the process demands, first, that no relevant judgment be suppressed, or more generally, that no assertive judgment at all be prima facie excluded from the process of inquiry. And it demands, further, that the guessing process, the process of potential hypothesizing, be considered always relatively incomplete as well as relatively complete. Both of these conditions, which are indispensable in defining explanation, and hence in determining the properties of any perspective in which explanatory validation can take place, have always been violated by dogmatic religion.

Yet, however misdirected a judgment may be, or however inapplicable and unfeasible it may be, its proper purview may be defined. Any judgment can be stripped of its pretensions and validated hypothetically. We can, for instance, specify the circumstances and assumptions by which any moral act may be justified. These may be utterly remote from the affairs that interest men, but for moral analysis and ethical speculation it is of utmost importance to discover such hypothetical justifications. They are guides to future conduct and stimuli to fresh appraisals of accepted standards, as well as indices to the completer understanding of actual judgments. As often as not, the circumscribed hypothesis which justifies may be contrary to individual and communal intent. The conditions that would validate an act for the individual's own perspective may be neither seen nor desired by him, though of course they must at some time be seen or desired by him if they are to be properties of his perspective. A religious dogma, stripped of its aspiration to pseudo-science, may have value as an exhibitive judgment, however much it may be abjured as such by religious devotees. It may function poetically in practice even if it be disregarded in theory; and if it be disregarded in both theory and practice by one religious community, it may yet, by the translation which query can effect, have value in the perspective of an alien individual or an alien community.

It may be argued that the validation of assertions depends upon the kind of evidence brought to bear, and that the kind of evidence brought to bear depends upon the interpretation that arises in a perspective. Thus it is sometimes argued by theists[12] that certain types of explanatory apparatus like that of science are limited to one kind of evidence and are unfitted to "see" what a theistic perspective would permit us to see, for instance theistic design and contrivance. The problem of evidence is a thorny one, both with respect to the definition of the concept and with respect to the interpretation of its instances. Nor can we ignore the fact that the alleged evidence for theism of one kind or another is psychologically compelling in many perspectives. And yet one thing seems clear. The compulsion effected by experimental investigation is inevitably universal, while the compulsion effected by theistic faith is not. Many of those who share a theistic perspective differ with respect to its implications, and even among those who concur the compulsion is as often as not intermittent and unpredictable. The conclusion indicated, whatever its meaning, seems to be that psychological compulsion of the so-called religious type is primarily a function of individual make-up, while experimental compulsion is primarily a function of discoverable relations among natural complexes. The type of precepts in the two cases is plainly different. There seems, it is true, to be no way by which a moral estimate of science and of universal compulsion can itself be made universal. Theists or scientists themselves may disparage the moral value of science or minimize the significance of its philosophic implications. But there is much less room to deny the differences between the perspectives of sanguine theology and the experimental spirit.

One thing, methodologically, can be said for the philosophic theologian. It is not he but the uncritical positivist who is inclined to oversimplify the problem of validation. The history of philosophy witnesses recurrent flights from the tangles of dialectic to the evidential authority of "experience," "verifiability," "testability." Failure to realize the different implicit usages, both common and philosophic, of terms like these, has allowed the opportunity for abuse in speculation and for theological pretensions to exactness. There are at least a dozen different major usages of "experience" in western thought, and to distinguish denotatively merely by saying, for example, that it is "experience" in the sense required by positive science that is fundamental is to exhibit a pattern of interest and not a methodology.

Nothing is more recurrent in the history of philosophy than methodological claims. The notion that one method, and hence one mode of validation, is superior to others is typical of every influential system. The Skeptics early attacked one aspect of all such claims by suggesting that no process of validation can be final in any absolute sense. Even pure mathematics, which in modern conceptions bases all demonstration on conventionally selected symbols and on stipulations, cannot exempt itself from the skeptical question whether we can be certain that all contradiction has been eliminated. We can have no final proof that our rules and symbols have been consistently employed. The laws of logic, which determine the process of consistent inference, represent the maximum compulsion in all query, but the question whether we are employing them properly, or even whether at some point the very compulsion to which we are subjected may not lead us astray in some sense, can always be asked significantly. The skeptical question, properly translated, is applicable to all modes of query. Whether any exhibitive judgment has most fully exploited its available medium, whether any human act could not have been wiser, more appropriate, or more humanly satisfying, is open to reasonable doubt.

Yet the question of relative superiority in method remains. Wholly aside from the issue of perfection in method, philosophic rivalry has been rich in boasts that one mode of validation is "real" or exclusive validation. The very number of these claims should offer grounds at least for suspicion that any one mode can exclude all others. One further result is suggested by the skeptical teaching, namely, that faith, in some minimal sense, is part of all query and all validation, even the surest and most advanced like pure mathematics. Faith, whatever its species, is relative confidence in what is unknown or unavailable—belief that a judgment beyond the pale of present validation, at best escaping from us Tantalus-fashion, is valid. In this sense, blind faith, the faith whose evidence can be equated with nothing more than hope or will, is different from other species only in degree. The magnitude of the degree that separates the mathematician or student of consistency from the fanatic is very great. But in the last analysis, one discerns a lot and the other little or nothing, while both feel equal, if not equally passionate, certainty. How is it possible to show that the progressive faith of the scientific attitude is superior to blind or partisan faith?

One elementary consideration imposes itself immediately, that the term "superior" cannot be used by itself but always requires the qualification "in such-and-such a respect." The expression "superior in all respects" is nonsense. The type of qualification required is one of evaluative choice or perspective. We might be implying: this is superior for me, for you, for the Eskimos, for an older tradition; or we might be implying: this is superior in terms of a specific order of judgments, a "point of view." It is easy to see that the former type of implication is an illustration of the latter. When we specify the moral or other grounds for judgments of superiority we are identifying a perspective in terms of which the value in question is affirmed. Superior "to me" means "in my proceptive domain." The perspective might be more limited. "Superior so far as I can see" may tacitly refer to the floating rather than to the gross domain.

To hold that progressive science is superior just because it is progressive and cumulative, because it promotes the ability to control, to manipulate, does not have the force that it is ordinarily made out to have. Methodological superiority, like any other, is relative to an end. If the end is control and prediction, then faith through critical selection of evidence is superior. If, on the other hand, the end is the development of aesthetic discrimination, or the intensification of a sense of holiness, or the nurture of apocalyptic expectation, then methodologically the technique and ruthlessness of blind faith may well be the superior means. Dedication to one end rather than another, and accordingly to one means rather than another, is a problem of moral choice, and cannot be dissociated from the proceptive direction. But to say that it is a problem of moral choice does not mean that it is an "insoluble" problem or that it is soluble only by each person for himself. For this would be to assume that individual query is completely autonomous—which we have shown to be patently implausible—and that communities of men do not have fundamental moral patterns which are communally binding and communally desirable—this, which we have not argued, we suggest is untenable and quite unimaginative. Moral similarity, the universal dominance of certain moral complexes, is a possibility for any kind of community. It may well be, then, that certain relatively pervasive ends among communities of men, ends which are desirable for them even if not presently and universally desired, are best promoted by one method rather than another which opposes it. And it may also well be the case, as I think it is, that the basic moral choices by which we justify one method like the scientific in the pervasive affairs of men are themselves validated in practice by that method, in company with complementary methods in other modes of query. Far from proving ultimate circularity, this would reinforce the concept of the (reciprocally describable) "connection" of judgments or sub-perspectives within a perspective. The moral and scientific perspectives within a larger human perspective would presuppose or imply or otherwise suggest each other, depending on the direction from which the larger perspective was explored.

In whatever ways the conflicting perspectival claims compare, one consideration is of prime importance philosophically, and hence morally—that the differences be recognized and acknowleged, separately from the need of the ego. Perhaps it is in this basic candor that the trait which men call reason ultimately lies. Reason, like method, is itself subject to perspectival interpretation, though it has been much more readily ascribed or denied than defined. Man himself has been defined in terms of it, and the life of reason declared to be his fulfillment. Reason and rationality have for the most part been explained denotatively, as though they resisted a direct approach. They have been located in the possession of knowledge, in the process of inquiry, in the state. They have been opposed to "faith," to "experience," to "intuition," to "chance," to "authority," to "superstition," to "force." On the other hand, some of these have also been held at one time or another to be parts or implements of reason; to be opposed to it only when championed independently; or to be, at least, consistent with it. Must reason be acclaimed inarticulately and without its saying something in behalf of its own essence? Is rationality ultimately a personal policy or habit, a local moral demand or proceptive bias? To say that practice and history implicitly determine its criteria is to say nothing clarifying, and even to abandon the problem to intuitively variable interpretations. To define it in terms of scientific method is at best to approximate it partially, and to omit from its domain, as irrational or non-rational or instrumental, other forms of expression and invention. To call it, with Santayana, "a harmony of the passions," is again, however true partially, to give it a psychologistic flavor that is surely inadequate.

The life of reason seems to be the life that not only has the capacity to pursue ends disinterestedly but is devoted to one overarching end as both a ground and a consummation of all values. This end needs to be morally and methodologically efficacious in the proceptive direction. It should be the essential element in "rational inquiry," "rational morality," and other specific rational allegiances. "Reasoning" or "rational insight" in their historical connotations do not furnish the key, for these, like the many complementary traits they have bred—"rational religion," "the light of nature"— are too narrow, confusing reason with truth-seeking alone. Reason is a form of love, as love (in an equally just perspective) is a form of reason. It is love of inventive communication. Nothing is more foundational for all value than query, and reason is devotion to query.

The qualification "inventive" is necessary. In communication as such there may be no good. It may degenerate into sheer coming-together, and in coming-together destruction is an equal possibility with invention. The rational spiral, in which communication generates judgments that promote communication, goes upward, not downward. The rational man welcomes the extension of his proceptive boundaries in the direction of invention. He is not just a seeker of "new experiences," for as merely new these may entail horror and death, but of experience which enriches query. War and disease and ill-will multiply communication quantitatively but defeat the worth of communication. Fear of invention—of communication lest it harbor products that demand query—is what we must mean by superstition. The rational man is willing to undertake the work of interrogation, since he implicitly perceives that the incompletion within life is perpetual and that the denial of query is stagnation and ruin. Reason cannot be a worship of the new; every moment bears newness, and mere persistence in time is no rational value. The problem of reason is to discriminate among the potentialities of the new. How can or how should it fulfill itself—that is, progressively achieve what it seeks? In the nature of the case, there can be no formula for either the achievement or the reward of rationality. It is for reason to discover and appraise itself from time to time and, like the god that it was early said to be, find that its work is good. Sometimes the progress of reason is more easily measured by the discernment of unreason and by the struggle that it is destined to undergo in order to prevent the fruitless death of its possibilities.

NOTES

1. John Dewey, *Art as Experience,* New York, 1934, p. 272.
2. W. M. Urban, *Language and Reality,* London and New York, 1939, Ch. VI.
3. Elsewhere I have sketched the significance for ethical theory of the concept of guiding tone. See the article on Russell's ethics in *The Philosophy of Bertrand Russell,* Evanston, Ill., and Chicago, 1944, Library of Living Philosophers, Vol. V.
4. Bertrand Russell, *Why Men Fight,* New York, 1917, p. 7.
5. C. S. Peirce, *Collected Papers,* ed. Hartshorne and Weiss, Cambridge, Mass., 1931-35, I, 170; *Philosophy of Peirce,* ed. Buchler, New York and London, 1940, p. 89.
6. Peirce, *Collected Papers,* V., 242; *Philosophy of Peirce,* p. 18.
7. Karl Britton, *Communication,* New York and London, 1939, pp. 131-32. Italics in the original.
8. W. E. Johnson, *Logic,* Cambridge, England, 1921, Part I, p. 94.
9. A. J. Ayer, in *Proceedings of the Aristotelian Society,* 1936-37, pp. 155-56.
10. The last few paragraphs are a modification of an article that appeared originally in *Mind,* October, 1939. My thanks are due the Editor for permission to use the material.
11. Cf. Peirce, *Collected Papers,* VI, 358, and V, 117; *Philosophy of Peirce,* p. 151.
12. Eg., A. E. Taylor, *Does God Exist?* New York, 1947, pp. 30, 34, 40-42.

APPENDIX

The pages and lines listed below locate words or phrases about which the following comments may be useful.

P. 5, line 13: *creation*. The term is used several times in this book. For a number of reasons I later came to prefer the term "invention." One reason is that "creation" suggests "excessive mastery of the producer over the product" (NJ 60). TGT and the later books make clear the unsatisfactory philosophic consequences of such a suggestion. (See, for example, CM 76–77 and ML 25–26.) Another reason is that "creation" somehow has become associated primarily with art, even with art alone. Yet, in order to avoid uncompromising departure from familiar locutions, I have made only a few changes in the text, so that both "creation" (or "creativity") and "invention" (or "inventiveness") are allowed to function synonymously.

P. 6, line 21: *object*. "Object" and "thing" are terms on which philosophers and non-philosophers alike rely for the purpose of general identification. Everyone at times needs to generalize unrestrictedly in this neutral respect. We speak of "any object we can describe" or "the things we worry about." Actually the reliance on these terms has handicapped philosophy, and especially metaphysics. It reflects, and perpetuates, an emphasis on space-time individuals as "ultimate." For it is extremely awkward and philosophically inept to speak of a political revolution, a convalescence, or a friendship as a "thing" or "an object." The situation is even more embarrassing conceptually when we need to speak in somewhat abstract terms, say of war, love, or gravitation, and are compelled to speak of them as "objects." The concept I have introduced to deal with this and other problems is "natural complex" (p. 7, lines 21–22). Whatever we wish to identify or talk about can be called a natural complex (or "complex"). Although the term is introduced and used in TGT, its philosophic function and significance are not dealt with in detail until MNC. [See also "On the Concept of 'the World,'" *Review of Metaphysics*, vol. 31, no. 4 (1978).] But once again, I have chosen to retain "object" in the text, because I wish to avoid an unrelenting use of terms which sound odd without adequate accompanying explanation.

P. 8, line 22: *perspective*. It is necessary to observe that the term "perspective" is not defined until chapter 5. The pertinent consideration here is that we should not think of a perspective as "in us." It would be more accurate to say that we are "in" a perspective, or that we occupy it; or, in the case of the proceptive domain, even that we "are" the perspective. (See comment below for p. 97, lines 7–8.)

P. 10, line 24: *complexity*. The relation and non-relation between my substantive term "complex" or "natural complex" and the adjectival use of the same word ("very complex," "far from simple") is discussed in MNC 24–25.

Pp. 10–11, lines 31–1: *proceives*. Since it is explicitly stated here that "proceives" is not a transitive verb, not an act that has an object, it may puzzle some readers to encounter phrases like "proceives nothing less than his world," "the world-unproceived and the world-proceived" (p. 25), or "nature proceived" (p. 28). These phrases are not meant to imply that the only object of proception is the world or nature. Quite the contrary, they are ways of referring elliptically and concisely to the ontological fact of man-related-to-his-world. "Nature proceived" means nature manifested humanly, or natural complexes being involved in a proceptive process. "The world-unproceived" means simply the world in so far as it is not humanly involved, not related to the human process. "Proceives nothing less than his world" means that what is defined as proception is the individual's comprehensive relation to the complexes of the world available to him.

P. 17, lines 3–4: *dimensions.* Some people are uncomfortable with the concept of dimension when it is used philosophically. They think of it as an overworked metaphor. Be that as it may, the concept is an extremely useful device for the characterization of inclusive complexes at any metaphysical level. It cannot be held responsible for its careless application. We may look at the matter in the following way. Anything can be said to have its "dimensions," in the etymological sense of measurable aspects. When we are concerned with complexes of relatively comprehensive scope, it is all the more desirable that their most significant generic aspects, their most fundamental "measurements," be conveyed conceptually. Thus, in the present system, manipulation and assimilation are dimensions of proception; compulsion and convention are dimensions of a human product's functioning; and on the broadest metaphysical level (see MNC, chap. 2), "prevalence" and "alescence" are dimensions of nature. Since "measurement" as such may be partial and yet useful, we can speak of dimensions even if we do not mean to speak exhaustively of "the" dimensions. The concept allows us to make important distinctions which combine an emphasis on contrast with an emphasis on complementarity.

P. 29, line 26: *Kant's*. Kant was not, of course, the only one or the first to use the metaphor of interrogating nature. What needs to be added, however, is that the concept of interrogation is far more fundamental than his system allows. It belongs, as our sequel shows, not to science alone (i.e., not solely to the process of inquiry) but to art and to purposive conduct of a constructive kind. It belongs (pp. 47–54 and passim) to all forms of query (see comment below for p. 54, line 1) and therefore to the inventive forms of exhibitive and active judgment no less than to those of assertive judgment. (See NJ, CM, and ML passim.) We can still say that we interrogate "nature." But nature can no longer be conceived as the subject-matter only of science. It is methodic man generally, and not just scientific or inquiring man, who interrogates. This means also (and the metaphysical ramifications are extensive) that "nature" cannot be narrowly limited to what is explored in behalf of "principles." Nature interrogated yields complexes for artistic and active judgment.

P. 34, line 19: *role-taking*. It is not my intention to dismiss or minimize the importance of the concept of role-taking, especially as developed by George Herbert Mead. The position here that role-taking is not an indispensable factor of communication recognizes at the same time the importance of Mead's views in the understanding of various aspects and circumstances of communication, as well as in the understanding of the relation between individuality and sociality. Mead's views, however, are not directly pertinent to what I regard as a *metaphysics* of the human process.

P. 40, line 9: *Adventure.* These lines are the fourth and last stanza of Emily Dickinson's poem numbered 822 in Thomas H. Johnson, ed., *The Complete Poems of Emily Dickinson* (Boston: Little, Brown, 1960).

P. 48, line 11: *concretizations.* This term in the singular is used here to designate no more than an instance of the emergence of a product. It could be used synonymously with "product" were it not required for the present expository purpose. But the term definitely is *not* intended to imply that all products are "concrete" in the sense of "tangible" actualities, nor indeed of actualities. Man produces possibilities as well as actualities. We say, for example, that medical research produces the possibility of a longer life span. The term "concrete," ironically enough, is one of the vaguest in the history of philosophy. See ML (chap. 3, "The Idea of Concreteness") and the article "On a Strain of Arbitrariness in Whitehead's System," *Journal of Philosophy,* vol. 46, no. 19 (1969).

P. 53, lines 6–7: *new life and growth.* New life and growth may be of a desirable or undesirable kind. See page 169 in the text.

P. 54, line 1: *query.* The concept of query is a fundamental one in the theory of judgment. It defines traits that are common to the different major forms of methodic judgment which are inventive in aim, e.g., art, science, moral conduct, philosophy. TGT introduces it in terms of its bedrock role as the benign form of methodic activity (though at times method as such is gratuitously assumed to be benign). It is greatly expanded in NJ and CM. The role of query as the interrogative temper manifested in poetry is described by ML.

P. 67, line 11: *assertive cognition.* Neither this phrase nor its context may be taken to imply that all knowing is assertive in character. On the contrary, knowledge may be equally acquired in exhibitive and active judging—though it is important to add that knowing is not the whole of judging, whatever the mode. This emphasis is rudimentary in TGT, and is made increasingly explicit in NJ, CM, and ML.

P. 97, lines 7–8: *order (perspective, context).* In the present chapter (4) these three terms are used more or less interchangeably, except where it is important to lay stress on the one that is most suitable for the statement of a general principle. "Order" meets this requirement, being here deemed the most generic of the three. It alone is appropriate for the most general ontological principles, or where the type of investigation is ontological. In this edition I have substituted it for "context" in several places. "Perspective" and "context" are forms of order. I favor "perspective" as more generic than "context," and more flexible, although both are abstracted or generalized from metaphorical uses. Perspective, as chapter 5 shows, is the kind of order in which man (a proceiver or society of proceivers) is involved. For the elaboration of the concept of order, see MNC.

INDEX

Absolute, 127 f.
Act, 46 ff., 64, 135, 152 f., 164; *see also* Active judgment
Active judgment, 48 ff., 64, 93 f., 110, 113 f., 120, 135 f., 138, 147, 149, 151 ff., 160
Adjustment, 17 f., 73
Allegiance, 42, 45, 67, 168
Ambiguity, 32, 137
Anthropomorphism, 37, 126 f.
Appearance, 15, 56, 107
Appraisal, 141, 150, 152
Appropriation, 11, 41, 52, 79, 149
Arbitrary convention, 97 ff.
Aristotle, 6, 46, 70, 74
Art, 21, 31 f., 52, 54, 66 ff., 73, 75 ff., 81, 92, 98, 102 f., 105 ff., 118 ff., 124, 133 ff., 142, 144 ff., 154 ff.
Articulation, 33, 35, 46, 65 ff., 120 ff., 133, 135 ff., 146 ff., 157, 159 f.; *see also* Commentative, the; Constructive, the
Assent, 77 ff., 121, 134, 150, 156
Assertion, 46 ff, 64, 67, 83 ff., 94, 137, 144, 152, 162; *see also* Assertive judgment
Assertive judgment, 48 ff., 64, 80, 93, 110, 113, 120 ff., 133 f., 136 f., 147, 149 ff., 155, 160 ff.
Assimilation, 17 ff., 25, 28, 51, 62, 74, 77, 136, 143, 155 ff., 169

"Basic" judgments, 82-89
Behavior, 4, 50, 127
Berkeley, Bishop, 30

Christianity, 42
Cognition, 67, 74, 78, 81 f., 108 f., 111, 134, 137, 143 f.
Commentative, the, 122 f., 133
Communication, 29-57, 58, 63, 65 ff., 75, 92, 113 f., 118, 123, 127, 135, 137, 139 f., 146, 153, 158, 168 f.; *see also* Reflexive communication
Community, 33-45, 51, 69, 77, 104, 114, 116 ff., 124, 132, 139, 166
Compulsion, 58-89, 90,, 101, 108, 110 f., 117, 131, 147, 150, 162 ff.; *see also* Evidential compulsion; Gross compulsion; Logical compulsion; Reflexive compulsion
Consanction, 91, 93, 96
Consciousness, 12, 50 f.
Constructive, the, 122 f.
Contrivance, 66, 107
Control, 73 ff., 166
Convenience, 91 ff.
Convention, 58 f., 90-112, 117, 130 f., 150
Criticism, 31 ff., 76 ff., 120, 131 ff., 137, 154 ff.

Democritus, 108
Descartes, René, 70 f.
Dewey, John, 25, 80, 106, 141
Discovery, 45 f., 66, 143
Drift, 22, 105

Empiricism, 11, 82
Encompassment, sense of, 81, 134
Epistemology, 12, 50, 57